Title: Living Diagnosis

Author: Blanche Haddow

Cover Picture by Blanche Haddow

ISBN-10: 1516835298

ISBN-13: 978-1516835294

Foreword
Tom Ramage

This is amazing.

Here's someone I've known half my life without knowing the half of it.

We shared four walls and three decades living two separate lives with one

result: half the story was told.

Reading the other half has been awesome – for both of us.

This book has clearly been a revelation for its writer as much as its reader

and that is what makes it so vital: no Dear Diary, not a redacted account

of a life lived but a running commentary, a wide-eyed self-analysis of a

reader more than a writer, desperate to discover what, why, how, who she

is.

Everyone should do this and I hope loads will follow her lead.

I can't wait to read her next thirty years. . .

Note

I just want to say thank you to everyone that has ever been in my life in any way good or bad as they have made my journey and me the person I am and I am very happy and glad to be that person.

Throughout the book I may have at times made some not so nice comments about people all as part of the journey and story. I want you to know that I love you all. It was important to me to keep the thoughts and feelings that are part of the story. No insult or offence was meant in any way. It also took me so many years to write the book that my views and feelings have completely changed in some ways. I have grown and learnt along the way but I tried to leave things as I felt and remembered them for the book. It was actually very interesting reading back over it and coming across memories that I knew but had forgotten. I definitely recommend having a go yourself at writing your own story.

I also want to make a point of thanking Dad and Sue (my step mum) for being with me and supporting me through many decades it is good to have parents that are there for you and I hope you both, and all of you, have enjoyed your own journeys.

Living Diagnosis

Quote through Dad by Aunty Ada: "Blanche was always a very strange wee girl, even before her Mum died."

Introduction

This book is a **living**, **evolving idea** for you to think about (A REAL LIVE CODE FOR **YOU** TO CRACK, SORT OUT and SOLVE).

You may be a therapist, academic, scientist, spiritualist, careers counsellor, an anybody or a nobody. Whoever you are and whatever you are, this book is for you.

We all place an incredible amount of trust and faith in professionals, doctors, therapists, psychiatrists etc. We open our souls to them and tell them our lives. Many of us, most of us would not tell these concerns, problems, worries, ideas to anyone else, no matter how close they might be. Well in this book **you** are the PROFESSIONAL and I am going to let you use me as a case study. In this way, it is a living, evolving book, a work in progress. **Your** thoughts, ideas, reactions and inputs can be listened to, collected, sorted and used to update and create new breakthroughs and advances in our world, society and the way we deal with, think about and evolve in our lives.

First of all let me tell you why this book is starting. Many times in my life, like a lot of us, I have thought about writing a book, even started writing a book. I've started different and even completed one writing course, Writing for Children, with chapter one of a book completed and a skeleton outline for the rest. A very good book it will be too, one day.

The trouble is these books, ideas and creative genius, rise up like a huge tidal wave. Swirl about in my head in the evening, get sorted out in my head as I'm **trying** to get to sleep, then that is it, they are finished. Finished and ready to start, but not done physically and they never see the light of day. Working on them after that would just be a chore.

Anyway back to why this book is starting. You will find that I jump from thought to thought. These 'jumps' are me, they are part of my brain or mind and the way I think. So the jumps will not be edited or sorted out, they are part of my make up and therefore important to you in your diagnosis.

Part 1

My Laziness

On Monday, I **had** to visit the Job Centre. I have kindly been assigned a Personal Advisor! These nice, friendly, approachable PAs are a huge improvement on the 'old' dinosaur, monsters, who looked at you and treated you like a very nasty, smelly piece of slimy stuff.

There was still one of these old relics from the past, when I first started my acquaintance with the Job Centre back in the 1990s.

The 1990s still seem very recent to me but I am beginning to realise that they were quite a while ago!

Attitudes, welcomes and atmospheres have all changed in today's modern (we're talking early 2000s here already out of date!) Job Centre. Sadly, the new 'upgraded' Job Centre may look swish but the atmosphere is not quite so nice. We now have security entrances, expensive 'glass cages' and uniformed men who I have been informed are Client Aides or something or other **not** Security Guards.

So I turned up to my Job Centre interview, praying to God and the Angels (my way of praying) that they would leave me in peace and I wouldn't have to get a job or go to the Support Training or Job Club place.

Many of you will describe me as a 'dole bludger' (well I reckon now that a lot of you would have a lot more colourful, fruitful language than that for it), that is ok. I believe we are all entitled to our own views and opinions. In fact for what that ('dole bludger') means, then I probably am. But don't throw the book away in disgust just yet. Remember that it is your job, with this book to 'listen' to the whole case, without judgement, and then with **all** the data and facts reach your own conclusion.

By the way 'dole bludger' may be a miss quote or the wrong words. You may find a few or a lot of them in this book. They are, again, a part of me and my case and therefore **not** to be edited. They just add to the colour and fun, a bit like Ethel (a clue to my age!!) did in Eastenders!

Well back to my 'PA' in the Job Centre. A peaceful life was not to be.

I'm actually a hard worker when I get going. I love doing things, paying attention to details and learning new things.

What I absolutely hate is feeling trapped. I think it is probably about control. It seems subconsciously that my way of staying safe is being in control.

My Dad (the loveliest Dad in the world of course) used to be quite strict when we were all at home. I have 2 older brothers and 2 much younger brothers, the 2 younger are technically my half brothers. My Dad and Step Mum gave us weekly jobs to do. As my big brothers got older, they used to have bad arguments with Dad.

We had to do, ironing, cooking, cleaning, gardening, babysitting etc and everything had to be done correctly. Dad would run his finger along the skirting boards and the top of picture frames to see if we had dusted properly.

One time my brother Duncan tore the linoleum when pulling the fridge out to clean behind it. Sue (our Step Mum) came home and spotted it straight away. We felt at the time that she must have been checking it to see if he had cleaned properly. Looking from a more positive note now, maybe it was just really obvious?!

We had loads of fun, silly songs and laughs along the way though. Perhaps those times are why I can't be bothered or have no motivation to do things now. I certainly do know how to work and work well and hard.

In recent years I have come to love gardening. I used to love just lying sunbathing but now I love being out working in the garden and making it look lovely. Perhaps it's just because I don't **have** to do it, that it is so much more enjoyable now.

As for housework, well I am much more lazy with that. My house is **never** unhygienic. I won't have food in the bedroom. That choice came after a noise in the night woke me up. I sat up put the light on and there in my slippers, sitting up looking at me like a hamster, was a rat (in reality apparently it was a mouse). I screamed and rushed to the door with the same thoughts of rapid escape as the mouse. My bare feet were jumping about like on hot sand, in case it ate my toes! I ran to Tom's (who owns my flat) bedroom door and shouted for him. The next day I moved back to my Dad's and refused to return until the 'rat man' had been.

I am allergic to cats and dust, well I was badly and think I still am, only I avoid them now as much as possible. So I always put off dusting and hoovering. Although that most definitely must have made the matter worse. Collecting collections (!), I always had **loads** of ornaments to dust under as well, not conducive to dusting motivation I can tell you.

My ornament collection is cut down a lot these days and my home is looking a lot cleaner. I created a saying 'IIDDINW' which I say whenever something needs doing. It works very well and means, 'If I Don't Do It No-one Will'. I'm actually getting quite good at cleaning although a bit lazy again now that I am back working, I would much rather go out and do my garden, which has become one of my more favourite activities. I hated gardening back at home when I was **made** to do it as a job. Sue had me picking dandelions out the grass with an old kitchen fork. Now forgive me Sue but that has to be one of the worst wicked Step Mum things you could have made me do!! I think the neighbours used to actually feel sorry for us and knew how much we had to do. I remember one time after seeing me trying to cut the grass edges with old useless sheers the neighbour lent me his electric strimmer, it was great fun.

But back to my ornaments, when I was younger, I always said that I collected collections. I'm not sure when it started although I always had ornaments and cuddly toys. I do remember going on holiday with my brother Duncan when I was about ten or so. We went to friends' friends, in one of the kids rooms, the boy had a collection of loads of tiny wee ornaments, funny wee things. After that I decided I wanted a room like that. Soon my collection built up. I always loved wee minature versions of things and remember tiny juice cans, I loved them and wee buggy cars.

The Buggy cars were really cute. I got them in a shop on my favourite holidays in North Berwick. There were different cars with names like Baby buggy, Sleepy buggy, Devil buggy, I'm not sure what the actual names were but I can picture the cars and the packets they came in. As far as I can remember, they were about an inch long, made of metal and plastic. Can anyone remember them? I would love to see them again. I remember being really disappointed when I couldn't get them anymore. I went into the shop in North Berwick and said "do you have the wee buggy cars that you used to have?" They asked me what I said, so I repeated myself. They thought for a while and then said "oh you mean these" and handed me a pack of miniature playing cards with bunnies on the back!! I suppose 'buggy cars' does sound very like 'bunny cards'! I've still got those bunny cards. I used to love playing patience and played many a game with them.

I often saw a collection of someone else's and thought that's brilliant, I want that. Like my brother Christopher's record (vinyl for you younger people!) collection and a collection of match boxes I saw in a cupboard at my Granny Roberts' that may have belonged to my Uncle John?

Granny Roberts for many years lived in the best house in the world at 3 Davidson Park Edinburgh. It had loads of rooms with cupboards and nooks and crannies. Upstairs was packed full of things left over from my Mum and Uncle John's childhood. There were old wooden floorboards with picture postcards varnished into them. A locked room with a flag hanging above the door that had the key in it. Loads of books and toys, a cuckoo clock and a secret passage way round to the other entrance to the locked room. I still sometimes have dreams about that house. Interestingly enough I once, as an adult, discussed that with my big brothers and they have those dreams too. In fact they also used to have dreams about secret doors and rooms there as well like in mine. Perhaps it is just a safe scene and environment in which to explore our lives, pasts, choices and ways forward.

My other collections that I can think of right now were, sugar wrappers, soaps, stamps, blazer badges, badges, coins, beer mats, smurfs (which in those days were called stroomphs (however you spell that) as they were from France. They changed the name when they brought them to Britain as they didn't think we would be able to say stroomphs.), snoopy books, postcards and I'm sure many more things that I can't remember right now.

Anyway back to cleaning. Although a messy person, it is a very ordered mess. I hate if someone moves an ornament or something and puts it back in the 'wrong place', I just have to sort it. Also I know where everything is or should be and am very good at finding things.

I loved to and was very good at finding things for my big brothers. They always said 'ask Blanche where it is' and I would very happily and with much glee find it for them.

So all of us Haddows like and need to be in control. This works fine until there is a difference of opinion. Luckily with us Haddows we are so cheery and daft that that (aren't double words strange things?) doesn't happen very often. Also luckily we all live in different houses now, more than about 2 days together can drive us all mad. Sadly we all mostly live in different countries as well now.

So I have learned to be someone who needs to be in control. Working 9-5 every day does not fit in with that and the thought of it feels more and more like a prison sentence. It is probably like a fear or phobia, the more

I avoid it the bigger and bigger the monster gets. Now it is really, really huge, it feels like it will just end my world to be stuck in a job I don't want.

So it wasn't nice when my Job Centre PA added: will do **any** job she is capable of. For 13 weeks or at the most 4 months, I have to go to the Job Club in Perth some days every week and every day for 2 weeks in July. That is not so bad, it is boring and pointless, I could do it all from home without having to get the bus into Perth. But I have been before and it is ok. It is actually quite nice to see and deal with people again and it is quite motivating **having** to look for and apply for jobs. But that is jobs that I want to do, or sound interesting or well paid. Not just **any** job.

I am hoping, really hoping, that I will get away with only applying for jobs that I want to. But I get a bad feeling about this, this time. Last time I was made to go for a job at a hair salon and then the threat of being made to go for a job in a burger van drove me to find a way to get to go to College. It worked and I got more qualifications to add to my collection and got left in peace for a few more years while I did what I really love doing, learning.

My qualifications are now:

Batchelor of Arts Degree in Child and Youth Studies (2001-2004)

SCOTVEC Higher National Diploma in Computing (1987-89)

SCOTVEC Higher National Certificate in Wildlife Habitat Surveying (1998)

SCOTVEC Higher National Certificate in Complementary Therapies (2001)

Associated Stress Consultants Diploma in Self Awareness (1996)

The New Age Foundation Diploma in Dream Analysis (1996)

(These last 2 are a bit embarrassing and I usually leave them out of applications so as not to add to my weirdness!)

I also now have quite a number of these training in service work things to add to the collection such as Child Protection, ECDL (European Computer Driving Licence) etc.

I can really struggle with education. I know that I am clever but I can't seem to get the marks. I sat Higher English and Higher Maths twice, I was amazingly even sent to private tuition for my Maths the second time but still got a C both times in both subjects. I never managed to get more than a C in English whatever the level. English teachers would probably recommend reading more books. But I have always loved and read books.

When young I had one of those black police books with the elastic to seal it and a mini pencil that fits in the side. In it I would list all the books that I read and then made a wee key to mark whether the book was (e)asy, (m)edium or (h)ard (or big). I was really proud if I read a 'big' book. As I am very good at finding things and knowing where they are or should be, I have just managed to find my wee black notebook. Here is what was in it for my book lists:

- = easy   x = ordinary   and   ✓ = big or hard
(See I nearly remembered the key correctly!)

Books I Have Read *(These ones must have been from about age 11)*

The Magicians Nephew x
Try it Again Charlie Brown –
A Bear Called Paddington –
Alberts Christmas –
The Voyage of The Dawn Treader x
You're a Winner Charlie Brown –
Hey Peanuts -
Who Was That Dog I Saw You With Charlie Brown -
Nobodys Perfect Charlie Brown -
Paddington Marches On -x
More About Paddington -x
Pollyanna x
Flambards In Summer x✓
Havelok The Warrior –x
This is Your Life Charlie Brown -
The Lion The Witch and The Wardrobe x
Here Comes Charlie Brown -
You're a Good Sport Charlie Brown -
Prince Caspian x
The Horse and His Boy x
The Silver Chair x
The Last Battle x
Charlie and The Chocolate Factory x
The Great Glass Elevator x
The Witch of Blackbird Pond x✓
The Search For Delicious x
Grump and the Hairy Mammoth –x
More British Fairy Tales x
Robinson Crusoe x
Boys and Girls Story Book –x
Proffessor Brainstorm x
Fattypuffs and Thinifers x

Books I've Read Since Christmas 1979 *(So I would just have had my 12th birthday)*

You've Done it Again Charlie Brown -
The Great Dragon Competition x
Gobbolino –x
Cider With Rosie x✓
Johnathon Livingston Seagull x
Black Beauty x
The Gypsy Tree x
Paddington –x
Happy Days x
Paul Mcartney and Wings x✓
Dads Army x✓
Charlotte Sometimes x
The House of Elrig x✓
The Bionic Woman x✓
Little Woman x
The Tinkers Wig –x
Sweet Thursday x✓
Young Wives x
The Thorn Birds ✓
Grange Hill x
Blue Peter Tenth x✓
Blue Peter Eleventh x✓
Blue Peter Twelfth x✓
Blue Peter Thirteenth x✓
Blue Peter Fourteenth x✓
Blue Peter Fifteenth x✓ *(I spelt that fiftheenth! And still couldn't spell it there when I tried. What a difficult word!)*
Buster Book of Spooky Stories -
The Black Island -
My Side of the Mountain x

Books I've Read Since Christmas 1980

Some Kind of Hero x✓
Vikings Dawn x
The Silver Sword x
As I Walked Out One Midsummers Morning x✓
Jessica on Her Own x
The Pigman x
The Siege of Trapid's Mill x
Devil-In-The-Fog x

13

My Bodyguard x
I am David x
The Lord of The Rings ✓ *(This was the 'proper' old yellow book where all the 3 books were together.)*
Argosy October x
Argosy September x
Oor John Willie x
A Spell of Sleep x
Then Again Maybe I Won't x
Argosy November x *(What on earth are these Argosy things??)*
Blubber x
Enchantment x
Argosy April x
Fifteen x
This School is Driving Me Crazy x
East of Eden ✓
The Little House on The Prairie x
Argosy February x
The Call of the Wild x
A Girl Called Al x
The Catcher in The Rye x
Smith x
Freeky Friday x

Christmas 1981

Alice in Wonderland and Through the Looking Glass x
Anne of Green Gables x
The Thirty Nine Steps x
Travels With My Aunt x✓
What Katy Did at School x
Tucker and Co x *(I loved Tucker Jenkins from Grange Hill!!)*
Autumn Term x
First Term at Trabizon x
The Day of the Triffids x
The Weirdstone of Brisingham x✓ *(I loved this one but remember never being able to say the last word, I still can't without reading it in front of me.)*
The Sword in the Stone x✓
Across the Barricades

Books I've Read in 1983

The Pearl
The Magicians Nephew *(Again! I did love my Narnia stories and spent many an hour sitting in wardrobes trying to get to Narnia!! (No I'm not joking!)) x*
The Lion the Witch and The Wardrobe x
Prince Caspian x
The Horse and His Boy x
The Voyage of The Dawn Treader x
The Silver Chair x
The Last Battle x
Grange Hill Goes Wild x
Kes x
Treasures of the Snow x✓
One Flew Over the Cuckoo's Nest x✓
Duty Calls x
The Cybil War x
Joby x-
Into Exile x
Iggie's House x
Zoo –x
To Kill a Mockingbird ✓
Jane Eyre x✓
Lord Foul's Bane ✓ *(I think this was the first of the Thomas Convanent books, that Christopher had. That got me started on my Fantasy Adventure books that I love and read non-stop still.)*
Grange Hill Rules ok x

Books I've Read in 1984
Animal Farm x *(That was most definitely a school book we **had** to read.)*
The Illearth War ✓
The Power That Preserves ✓
The Wounded Land ✓
The Great Gatsby x
The One Tree ✓
The Prime of Miss Jean Brodie x
White Gold Weilder ✓
Sunset Song x
Being There *(I talk about this book later.)*
The Secret Diary of Adrian Mole –x
The Growing Pains of Adrian Mole –x
Crowdie and Cream x

Books I've Read in 1985

The Rainbow ✓
Wuthering Heights x
The Land of Many Colours ✓
A Childhood -
Fortunoff's Child ✓
The Once and Future King ✓
The Book of Merlin –x
The Complete Knowledge of Sally Fry x
Welcome Home Jelly Bean x
It's Not the End of The World x
Crotal and White x
Claudine at School x
All Girls Together x
Martin Minton -

1986 *(Now just turned 18 I must have finally got bored this year of writing down the books!!)*

Nicholas Nickleby ✓
Onions in The Stew x
A Town Like Alice x

So you can see, I meant it when I said that I read loads and loads of books as I grew up. That list fair brought back a lot of memories. It's a funny mixture. You can see when I started to look around the house for books and read whatever I could find. I like the way I have graded them it must have been difficult to make up my mind what mark they would get at times! I've no recollection whatsoever of all those Paddington books, maybe they were out of the library? As you can see I did (do) have a lot of snoopy books in my collection! Hidden away in a box now, it would be nice to get them out and read them again. They would have to go in the deep freeze first though! Someone once told me about the freezer killing the dust mites. I wrap an old book in a bag and put it in the freezer (I've only got a freezer compartment of the fridge) overnight. It works a treat, gets rid of that old musty smell and leaves the books lovely and fresh and even clean seeming.

I obviously haven't written down all the books, I can think of quite a few we did at school that aren't on that list. Perhaps I only wrote down the ones that I chose to read myself? I always remember really enjoying books at school until they made us analyse them. For me, books are about the magic, getting lost in the story not picking them apart. That really spoils the flow for me. My friend Babs and I really enjoyed the nice story about animals when reading 'Animal Farm' at school until they started telling us it was all about the Russian Revolution

aaaaaaaaaaaaaaaagh!!

I love books that I can get 'lost in'. An Educational Psychologist whom I got a dyslexia test from at College got confused when I said 'lost' in books. He explained that he deals the whole time with people who get lost while trying to read. Of course that is not how I meant it. I get 'lost' in the story I become part of it, hear the sounds and feel the feelings. More on that later and also more about that Educational Psychologist.

I read Lord of the Rings when I was still quite young. In those days all 3 books were together in one big yellow covered book. It was suggested to me that I read the Hobbit first as it started the story and was easier to read. So of course I didn't and went straight on to The Lord of the Rings. I still haven't read the Hobbit and guess that I should someday. I never read Enid Blyton either because everyone always said they were great, I just wasn't interested. It's strange as I bet that I would have loved them.

Later I really got into Fantasy Adventure books after reading my big brother's books, The Chronicles of Thomas Covenant. They really got me hooked. Stories that I could get lost in! Aha, you may say, that's where she went wrong no 'proper' books. But while growing up, at home (my

Dad's), I would read every book that I could find. I learned a lot about life from those books like The Thorn Birds but also authors such as Laurie Lee, Lewis Grassic Gibbon, and Steinbeck etc. I remember learning what 'crap' meant from one Steinbeck (I think) book when a man was caught while in the loos having a 'crap'. My motto was and still is never to give up on a book no matter how dull it may be. I do confess on giving up on, I think it was, the Old Curiosity Shop. I was very disappointed in myself as the title sounded really interesting. I expect that the old dusty copy didn't help. I can smell when I am going to be allergic to a book, that old musty, dusty smell and look gives it away.

Another one I had to give up on was an adult C.S. Lewis one, I found it far too slow going. Again I was really disappointed especially since I had loved the Narnia books so much. I spent my childhood sitting in cupboards waiting to get to Narnia! By the way I would like to make it known to the World that the Magicians Nephew is the first Narnia book not The Lion the Witch and the Wardrobe like everyone seems to think. That sort of thing is very important to me!

Having to give up on a book reminds me of a thing that I once saw on tv. I put the television on and there was an extremely strange scene of 2 people buried up to their heads in sand talking to each other. For some reason I watched it for a bit maybe to see what on earth it was? I remember it being so boring but I kept watching just to see when it would change scene but it just kept going. It got to the stage where I felt so annoyed at having watched so much that I didn't want to stop as then it would be like giving up and a complete waste of time, so I carried on!! I think that I did give up in the end when really driven to boredom. I wonder if they ever did change the scene. I've no idea what it was but I think my Dad has told me in the past what it would probably be as it sounds like a particular writer's work. I will have to ask him again what it might have been. (He thinks it might have been Happy Days Samuel Beckett.)

So where was I? Oh yes education. My BA in Child and Youth Studies really suited my learning style well. It was carried out using the Internet. I based myself at Perth College library, so each day I went into a nice, quiet but interesting environment. All the books, computers, data etc were on hand. This way, while I was there I worked and I stayed whole days as an, only hourly, bus journey back to home meant that there was no chance of nipping home or going off and doing something else. No distractions like computer games, people phoning or anything. I hate phones. In my opinion sales people phoning should be illegal! And mobile phones should all be put in a huge pit and blown up! I expect if I gave in to a mobile phone I would soon be as addicted as the rest of human kind. I plan to learn to drive (positive thinking here) and I think a mobile phone in the car would be a very wise idea for breakdowns etc, which is quite funny as that is the one place in the world where mobile phones are actually banned! Yes I know it's for a different reason but it's still ironic. I think it is hilarious when people are in a cubicle in the loo talking to someone on their mobile phone and people walking along talking to someone on hands free phones sound so silly as well. In fact them being on the phone in the next loo cubicle can also be very annoying and embarrassing, I would like the choice whether the sound of my wee will be heard by extra people or not!!

I remember going into the local corner shop and going up to buy my 'pint' of milk. The shopkeeper said, really nicely, "hi how are you". So I answered her "fine thank you". It was much to my embarrassment, a second later, when I realised that she was actually talking on her mobile phone. I find that sort of thing really rude and confusing although they are not at all meaning to be rude.

The ladies in the office at Perth College when I worked before in D.T.P (Desk Top Publishing), soon realised that it was much easier to avoid having me answer the phone. I would be that busy trying to work out how to spell the persons name that I would leave half the address out to fill in later and of course once I put the phone down I'd forgotten completely what the bits I missed out were. I was ok at remembering the message but an anonymous message, wasn't exactly handy.

It is interesting, I think, that it was things like names that caused me problems, words that I couldn't picture and so had to think about the sound to spell. I can't do that really. With a strange word it often means that I don't actually know what a person is saying. It is much easier for me if someone says an unusual word to ask the person to spell it or write it down. I then understand what they are saying. Otherwise it can be, at times, like I can't make sense of the sound.

When in France visiting a family friend, Arlette, I remember her trying to tell me the French word for ladybird, coxinelle. I just couldn't work out what she was saying. So she gave me the letters and suddenly I could hear it and make sense of it, what's more I can still remember it which is amazing for me. I just looked it up and it is actually coccinelle, which is actually even more interesting as I have remembered how to say it but not how to spell it, even though it was the spelling that got me the sound in the first place.

So the learning environment, for my BA studies, suited me brilliantly. With no classes to skive from it was up to me to prioritise and motivate myself to get the work done. Coming into College each day to my computer worked really well. The fact that the work was all online suited me perfectly as well.

In College before, with traditional type courses, I found it impossible to concentrate on the lecturer just talking on and on for a whole lesson. I'd do a wee (By the way because I'm Scottish, I say wee for little, much to some peoples' amusement, but smiles are good!) game that when they said "more about that later", I would try to concentrate enough and for long enough to actually hear when they did get back to that topic. I don't remember ever actually hearing them getting back to that point nor actually even remembering what the original point had been anyway. But the challenge did get me managing to listen and concentrate for longer than I would have done. Another thing I learnt was that if I took notes then I had no idea what had actually been said and found it really boring when I had to read through the notes later to study, it just didn't work. Sometimes my friends would laugh if they borrowed my notes as every now and then, to make the reading more interesting, I would change ink colours or write, 'keep going Blanche you can do this', or 'this is so boring'.

Something that worked better was when I really concentrated on the lecturer but then of course I had no notes for later study. I expect it would be much easier for me nowadays, in this technological age, where there would probably be lecture notes available electronically before and after each lecture. I would be able to print them out, read them if I was good, and then use highlighters (to keep me interested) and write short mental hint notes on the printed out sheets.

So working on the Internet suited my learning style a million times better than my earlier classroom based lessons. I love using computers and can use them for hours. I always feel that when you find something that you can get 'lost' in for hours, like I do with painting, reading and computing, then that is what you should do as your career.

The work was written on the screen with different colours, fonts, text sizes, and pictures and to get into it and move and work through it I had to take part. It was interactive and I loved that. It kept me much more motivated and interested.

There was still the problem in some subjects where part of the work was to read through great chunks of textbooks. My Step Grampa helped with that, in telling me how to 'skim read'. The trick is to read the first paragraph, then just the first sentence of the main text and the whole of the summing up paragraphs. This worked a treat for me. Thank you 'Grampa Stan'. What a breakthrough, I was now able to read through all the necessary reading quickly (for me), quite easily and actually know what I had read about, be able to take part in 'discussions' on the matter and usually even find it interesting. Whereas before, reading text books would have taken me hours, I would only read about a page or two, give up in complete boredom and despair and have no idea what I had just spent all that time reading.

Although Internet learning really suits me I still had the problem that I've always had of thinking that I know what is being asked for. Doing and enjoying all the work and then finding out that everyone else has known (I've no idea how) to do it in a completely different way and that I haven't actually answered what was asked for, aaaaaagh.

That 'aaaaaagh' reminds me that I hate when authors write sounds in books. They never look like what I think the sound should be like. I remember reading a book where the author kept putting what was supposed to be the sound of the horse but to me it was all wrong and it stopped the flow of my reading. This of course stopped the magic of me getting lost in it. I suppose that if, in my head, I begin to hear the sounds of the story and get lost in it then a wrong sound or a sound in the wrong place would stop me in my tracks.

Sometimes I wonder if I don't hear the beginning of words. My nephew Jack (more about him later) when he was young, for a while, had a 'language' that only his Dad and Mum could decipher. I noticed that he would miss out the middle of words like 'hos' instead of 'horse'. But for me it seems, for listening, to be the starting sound that I can miss.

When I worked for the Wildlife Trust the other volunteers would tease me for saying, what they said was 'cheese' instead of 'trees'. As you can imagine with Wildlife Habitat Surveying the subject of trees came up quite a lot. But I couldn't hear that at all and am still adamant that 'trees' is what I actually said!

My Dad was given a 'brain gym' game along with a Nintendo DS for a Christmas present one time. He had a couple of shots of it but gave up because the machine couldn't make out some of the words that he was saying. That is probably to do with his Scottish accent and it is very annoying, it makes me shout at the machine even louder! (A bit like some of us do to foreign people thinking that will make them understand better!) It is amazing what these computer game things can do these days and we should really be stunned and extremely impressed at what it can actually do. But anyway that wasn't what I was going to discuss. It was that when I had a shot of the game it kept saying "wrong" when I was saying a particular colour, I can't remember if it was red or yellow? Anyway my brother Calum said that I kept saying the word funny, I didn't believe him and had no awareness of saying it wrong whatsoever but the machine did keep not recognising the word.

Anyway back to not answering the question in my studies. By the end of my degree I began to learn the trick of working with the question and study points to work through and answer in the way that was required. Not in the way that I felt the approach and answer should be. I struggled a lot more in second year and much preferred third year where the mark weighting allowed much more for our own thoughts.

I understand that we need to learn and understand the background and also accepted the comments that it would be useless not to know and study previous research or there would just be repetition and wasted time. But to me I feel that it should be about thinking and developing ideas, trial and error rather than endlessly repeating and discussing the pros and cons of old ideas and theories. An example of this, that began to drive me mad, was the Nature/Nurture debate. It has all been discussed and debated before. Things, views and ideas change and evolve with new breakthroughs and understanding but what does the actual question matter? I know that genes or environment etc are important in their effects and what we do/don't do for development but why go over the same ground again and again. Why not just know these things accept the different possible sides and balances then get on with new radical ideas and experiments.

Another repetition that really annoys me is when there is a big news story or disaster and it is repeated and focussed on over and over. I hate the way nowadays these events seem to be made into entertainment, with special presenters, big screens and statistics all quickly developed for the 'show'. It is not that I am heartless, that I don't want to watch disasters. In fact it is the opposite, I feel them too much. They make me feel ill. Once I have heard and seen the facts then that is it. For me it doesn't need to be repeated over and over and on and on.

The getting on with new things for experiments is how I feel about such things as the dolphin research and the scientific way of doing and looking at things generally.

Dolphins are obviously highly intelligent. Research has already shown that they cannot only understand human signs for such things as bucket, hoop, ball etc but they also understand the differences in sentence structure. So they understand the order in which the signs are given.

I got interested in studies and working with dolphins because of the amazing work that has been done with children with Autism and various animal therapies. Horace Dobbs has written a number of interesting books about his experiences and work with dolphins. You can find more information about it all at the International Dolphin Watch website:

http://www.idw.org/

So why not just accept that? I mean about the dolphins being highly intelligent and being able to work with communication, and not spend millions more pounds and years doing more of the same types of simple experiments. Why not start new research into us trying to use and understand their language or what they would do or choose to do to teach us. I'm sure that the dolphins must get bored (to put it politely) of the same old experiments as well. Although it must be nice for them to, at least in a very basic limited way, have us humans actually communicating with them. I am not meaning to be anthropomorphic (had to look that one up!) here. I'm just trying to make a point about their intelligence and how we may be wasting time dealing with them in such an extremely basic manner.

(I have just been reading in the SpeakDolphin website:

http://www.speakdolphin.com/home.cfm

about how research is moving on with new digital recording capabilities that are now able to really capture and analyse dolphin sounds. This all sounds much more like it and very interesting research.)

It fascinates me how although these wild creatures may snap off over friendly humans' fingers or bruise a person to the point of drowning, that they can then realise when a human isn't coping, is in trouble or when a young child with special needs, requires more care and gentle attention.

I'm a spiritual person, not religious. I don't believe that is should be about rules and regulations but love and light. Now then before I lose another huge batch of scientists or people with certain religious beliefs, remember, you have to get all the background before you can make your diagnosis.

When scientific minded people write off whole areas of thought and exploration just because there is no 'proof', it seems to me so stupid and such a waste. It seems that a person can be highly intelligent but have hardly any wisdom.

So, back to my job search, well this time I've no possible way left to fund any more education. It really annoys me on the TV on things like Millionaire when they talk about how a person has to pay off the huge student debts of thousands of pounds that they have run up. They say it as if the student had gone out partying non-stop and wasted all their money away. Well maybe they did party but I can assure you that it would have been at discount drink party night type doos.

To me it seems perfectly fair that we pay for our degrees the way we do, not paying it back until we get a well paid job and then only in bits each month as we can and that it cancels out if you die or reach retiring age. I see this system as reasonable and fair. But what isn't fair and what you don't hear about is the interest that is building up, even while still studying, and on and on if you don't get a job and can't start paying it back.

Another thing that wasn't explained and I feel should have been is that for the last 3 years of my studying I should have been paying National Insurance. Obvious perhaps, but if I'd realised I probably at the time could have paid that wee bit each month instead of getting a letter afterwards warning that I had a few hundred pounds to pay. By this time, of course, I was back to being unemployed. Being long term unemployed means you have no savings and no spare cash. It drives me mad when people say I've no money but they **actually** mean I've a savings account or two, a car, a house but I've no spare cash to spend at the moment.

It should be pointed out here that I am extremely careful with money and have never been in debt or overdrawn in my life. I don't believe in credit cards, if I don't have the money then I shouldn't spend the money. I'm very frugal, living on unemployment benefit makes that a necessity, but I am anyway. When I had money I would occasionally go a shopping spree to cheer myself up, a brilliant therapy. However I wasn't the sort to splash out on designer things, I don't use handbags, makeup, high heels etc. My idea of heaven shopping is things like bubble bath and I really love buying books and looking in bookshops.

I've found that now that I am working again in a well paid fulltime job I can't get back into that treat I used to love of occasionally going on a shopping spree to cheer me. I don't know if it is because I have become stingy or rather more careful with my money and things are ridiculous prices now. I am not interested in spending more than about £20 on a piece of clothing and have no idea why we should unless of course it was all manmade and handcrafted or something like that. Also I was so long without money that I haven't really bought new clothes for about 20 years, I never was very fashionable, and now I just find the fashions and styles so ridiculous and silly looking that I am not interested even if they didn't cost so much money.

I do like some of the styles and ideas in a shop called 'fat-face' but I reckon that the prices, even with a sale, are, again, completely ridiculous. I have a theory that the company should set up a shop next door to every 'fat-face' called 'thin-face' and have the same clothes with really cheap prices. Then the people who care about money and 'like' to spend lots of money on their clothes can still go to 'fat-face' and the people who want a good quality bargain and don't care about the label as long as they get the style and quality, can go to 'thin-face'. In 'thin-face' the company would make such a multiple extra number of sales that it would more than make up for the drop in prices!

In fact this would be a really interesting experiment into the effect and influence of labels on consumer buying. They would have to be very careful though, as I reckon that within 10 years the 'young' people who love the labels would have grown up and had to buy their own clothes and realised that it is not really worth it to pay £50 for the exact same product when they know that it was made by the very same people using the very same materials. I know at the moment people pay for quality and the way of judging that quality is by the label or maker. But what if the item and maker was exactly the same and only the label and price were completely different?

I wonder if perhaps I have gone lazy with my shopping as well. I am a fit, healthy person who loves to go outside and walk every day but I just can't be bothered trailing round shops and lugging shopping bags around and home on the bus anymore. I have started to shop on the internet for some things. Which is great for finding out about the different choices and prices and also for reading reviews and views about the items. It's not good though, for me, for things like clothes and food as I am so extremely fussy that I like to actually see the item in front of me and check whether the ham has 'fatty bits' in it or whether the material of trousers is horrible clingy stuff.

With my love of buying books, I have got into the habit of looking for and buying books on Amazon which is brilliant but I do feel really bad and guilty and scared at times that it means I am adding to the demise and downfall of the brilliant, wonderful, good old bookshop. I would hate to lose them even though I never actually go to them much these days.

Over the years I have tried a number of times sending letters and my CV to bookshops such as Waterstones, where I would love to work. I reckon I spoiled it after the first time though, when I was still just a young thing! I amazingly got invited in for an interview after writing a letter to Perth Waterstones. The interview was going well until the lady asked me what books I was reading at the moment. I, without thinking, said "oh I can never remember the actual name of the books". She very nicely didn't laugh out loud but I didn't get invited back! It's true though, I wouldn't be able to tell you a book title or author, but if you told me what it was about, I would be able to show you exactly where on the book shop or library shelf you would find a particular book from the picture in my head.

The authors and titles just don't stick in my head, they are not important to me for my reading of the book (unless I want another book by an author that I enjoy of course). I also, I suppose, don't make the effort to get the words into my memory as I have no reason to. When I'm reading a book, I try really hard not to look at the picture on the cover as I don't like when a picture in the story is made for me by someone else, it spoils my imagination. I also feel that way about seeing characters in films before I've read the book as I then can't help but picture them in the story and it is not what I would have pictured them to be like.

I sometimes feel it doesn't say much for my life that I own nothing, no car, no house etc. But I am not that bothered about material things. Money is handy and great fun, I'd love to win the lottery (and will of course) but I'd much rather be free to do my own things and enjoy my life than work 9-5 just to have money.

Dad tells me that he used to be the sort of person that saved and invested all his money for the future but then my Mum died of Cancer at the age of 36. He asked a doctor in the hospital, after it happened, 'what am I going to do now'. The man told him to get on with his life and enjoy it. Dad felt after that, that it was much better to enjoy life and put people first before money. He says that he taught us that. I don't remember in anyway being directly taught that but it obviously must have had a big effect on my life judging by the way I am now.

Isn't effect a funny word? No matter how many times I am told or read and think I've worked out the uses and difference between effect and affect, when it comes to writing it I am never sure which to use. I find it best to just write or say it and see which of the 2 words arrives naturally! I don't know if that works though!?

So my student loan was £3000+ something, times 3 years and with interest is mounting up at a dramatic rate. The way I look at it though is it's not a real debt in that I don't have to pay it back until I can. The couple of hundred times three, for the National Insurance is something that I will pay back as soon as I can, I reckon some money will come my way soon enough. I will win a competition or something.

(I am going through this book and updating it as I check or read it. It turns out now that they have changed the National Insurance system and I will be all right with the years I have missed but will just have to be very careful in the future. Now that I have a good full time job I get a part of my wage taken out each month to pay back my Student Loan but I have also arranged to pay back £50 a month to try and bring it down at least to the state where the interest that they are adding on each month is getting cancelled out even if the actual amount I owe is not going down much.)

I'm a positive thinker. Life's good and cheery that way. When I, out of the blue, got a bill for £1000 for student tuition fees, I said to my friends

"I need £1000 but I don't have it, don't worry I'll get it." Another of my mottos is, 'have trust and faith.'

Next thing I knew I heard that I had won £1000 in a magazine (Chat, IPC Media, Issue 14 3/4/2002) competition! What's more it was a lovely way to win it. 'Ruth The Truth' had drawn a simple picture of an object and we had to guess what it was and draw it. Apparently there were thousands of entries and my simple picture of a flower had come closest to it. It was a brilliant way to win a competition and also really handy just when I needed exactly that much money.

I really love going in for competitions and would love to be one of those professional compers. That would be a bit too serious for me though and really take the fun and excitement out of it. After winning my first couple of prizes of insect repellent(!!) I have won a few things. I started making a list, it's not like the great expensive, amazing lists of the true compers but it's not bad:

4/7/01	Lottery £10
June 2001	MosiGaurd Stick
5/11/01	MosiGuard Roll-On (After this I realised that it wasn't always good to win things if you didn't actually want them!!)
8/1/02	Psychic Quiz £1000 (Chat) (My favourite win.)
11/2/02	Bath Towel 'Nice n Fresh'
7/8/02	Original Source 2 Deodrants,2 Shower Gels
27/11/02	£10 Thedailydraw.com
16/1/03	Andrex Puppy Cuddly Toy
12/9/03	Extra Month Subscription for Compers News (Slogan: You know you are a true comper when . . . 'the price of a stamp matters'.) (I used to love doing my compers magazines every month, filling out all the postcards and envelopes, sticking on stickers and sending them all away in the post. Unfortunately slowly they started filling them up with phone and website competitions and it just wasn't worth getting the magazines anymore.)
13/9/03	New World Music 2 CDs, Reiki Music and Guided Meditation for Sleep (Through Chat magazine.)
March 2004	£5 Amazon Internet Voucher, Internet Survey Calicado
April 2004	£2 Shopping Voucher, Consumer Club
March 2004	£2 Shopping Voucher, Consumer Club
29/7/04	Chat Reader Puzzle Creation £20 (I liked doing that one. I was amazed how difficult it was to make a tiny wee letter puzzle.)
7/8/04	Book 'The Home Buyers Guide' (I wonder what I did with that I don't remember it at all.)
19/3/05	£4 O'Lucky Day Scratch Card

21/3/05	£4 and £8 O'Lucky Day Scratch Card (Oops I bet that got me into scratch cards for a while!)
2/4/05	£10 Lottery
13/5/05	£5 Amazon Voucher Internet TV Questionnaire (I used to love doing this survey as I won Amazon vouchers quite regularly and was able to treat myself to books but sadly the prizes died down a lot and I gave up with it.) (I'm back to it these days and have won a few small Amazon token prizes)
July 2005	£5 Amazon Voucher Internet TV Questionnaire
24/9/05	Lottery £10 (I didn't do the Lottery as a matter of principle for a long time after it started. But one day in the bakers a lady said to me well you won't win anything if you don't try. So I decided to give it a go. Now I buy one ticket for a Saturday each week and limit it to that. I always have the same numbers. I know they say that it is completely random and so there is no point in doing the same numbers but of course there are also the laws of chance. I haven't had tails on my coin for many months so it must be due very soon! I believe in positive thinking and creating what you believe in. So I am going to win the Lottery. I am going to win £2 million. It used to be £1 million but it has gone up with the price of inflation!)
8/10/05	Loaf of Hovis White Bread, Somerfield Swipe (I don't know what I did with that one, I only like brown bread. I probably gave it to my friend Babs.)
24/10/05	£5 Amazon Voucher Internet TV Questionnaire
15/11/05	Flake, Somerfield Swipe (I don't like chocolate either!)
18/11/05	£5 Amazon Voucher Internet TV Questionnaire

6/12/05	Schuh Mag Babycham Velcro Graffiti Trainers (I like these and still have them in the cupboard although the soles are getting a bit worn now.)
1/4/06	£10 Book Token Lightspeed Internet Panel (When I was unemployed, I had loads of time to do all these internet questionnaires, I can't be bothered these days.)
5/4/06	£5 Amazon Voucher Internet TV Questionnaire (I told you that I won a lot of these!)
13/4/06	Kids Dance Mat (I thought that I would use this as good fun exercise but I only used it about once, I ended up taking it to the Comrie Kids Club when I worked there.)
27/7/06	Two Tennis Rackets and Balls, ITA Advantage Club (This was a really good prize and my nephew, Jack, and I actually took them down to the park and had a game with them a couple of times.)
21/8/06	£10 Boots Gift Voucher, Pringles Dippers
24/8/06	Rapidough Board Game (I really like this game, you have to make things out of playdoh, great fun but I've only managed to play it about twice as no volunteers!)
22/9/06	Postman Pat Memory Game (This one got donated to the nursery beside the Comrie Kids Club.)
27/1/07	Winning Moves, Double Quick Word Game, Chat Magazine Issue 46(2006) (Another good game that I've only had the chance to play a couple of times. I live on my own. I love the freedom and chance to do what I want when I want but it does get very lonely at times.)
22/2/07	Book 'Hope'
January 2009	Two Pig Torch Keyrings, Perth College Raffle

January 2009	Box of Bath Stuff, Raffle, Quiz Night (I love going to quiz nights, especially with my pal Babs, her husband (Graham) and brother (Andrew). We are getting better at them, although we hardly ever get to go. I can never answer much but I do always astound people with my knowledge of strange things that no one else knows.)
28/11/09	£10 Lottery
31/1/10	£10 Lottery, Lucky Dip (As you can see I did stop doing my competitions nearly so much but I do still occasionally get back into the swing of them.)

Although I have my £1000s student debt, I am very careful and sensible with money. It is very hard to live from unemployment benefit. In fact it's quite a job in itself trying to manage.

That reminds of me of one time on the television when a very brave Conservative (I think) young man politician, tried to live on benefits for a week, taking the life of a young Mum. It was a very interesting programme and showed how hard it was. But what they didn't show or realise was that it started with staple items already in the house. Try reducing your benefit by the few pounds that it takes to buy simple items such as toilet paper, rice, washing machine liquid etc, the worse things are toiletries such as sanitary wear, deodorant, hair removing things etc and also they don't think about such things such as birthdays and Christmas, which can become almost impossible (even if you are careful with how much you spend) especially if you have a large family.

So I don't reckon unemployment, even without all its' stigma, would actually suit many people.

I never go nights out, holidays, buy household items etc. I can't really afford clothes except when really necessary. It is a big problem at certain times of the year like June when the phone bill is due and also I have 3 peoples' birthday presents to buy or at Christmas.

(I'm glad to say that now I have a good job and can afford things again. It is really nice to be able to get things again without worrying. I've even treated myself to an electric piano. I've always wanted a piano. I bought an electric one so that the volume could be adjusted so the noise wouldn't annoy the neighbours so much. I really love it and have got myself a DVD course to work through and learn how to play. The lessons really suit me and are well worth the money as I can play each lesson over and over as much and often as I need and the teacher never gets annoyed! My plan is to one day be able to play Moonlight Sonata by Beethoven. See working does have its good points!)

I like to eat a good balanced diet. Though money wise I often stick to things like pasta and vegetables. (Again that was written when I was unemployed. Mind you the prices of food now are incredibly silly and high. My shopping bill has at least doubled since just a few years ago due to price increases. I was stunned one time the other month to find a small tub of raspberries on sale for £4. I didn't buy them! So I've no idea how I would have managed now with the new food prices with the money that I was living on then.)

Living well, getting out and about every day (no matter what the weather) and eating well are very important to me. I don't believe that any one food type should be cut out completely. It also seems to me, **much** more sensible to get all the vitamins and minerals that we need (where possible) from fruit, vegetables and the rest of our food rather than supplements. There is a problem with that in some ways for instance with Omega3 oils, I don't like oily fish. I really wish that I did, as it is obviously really good for you, but I don't. Apparently walnuts are a source though and I love nuts, and eat them mostly every day (unsalted now that I have gone healthy!).

Starting to have sore thighs or knees in the night when it is really cold, I decided to start trying cod liver oil. I started with the capsules but was worried about the ingredients as they all seemed to have added Vitamin A and D in them. What is the point of adding synthetic vitamins to a substance that already naturally contains the same vitamins naturally? Apparently the body can cope with the excess natural vitamins but isn't able to get rid of the synthetic ones. I even tried pure cod liver oil liquid as that didn't have anything added. I thought how revolting can it be? But it was revolting, like the idea of swallowing the linseed oil that Dad has always kept in the garage for his wooden handled tools. So I went back to the capsules and thankfully, I have now found some that **don't** have any added vitamins.

I have cut down with salt in cooking for boiling things I use lime juice instead which works a treat. For cooking things like mince, I use fish sauce instead of salt, hopefully getting a wee bit more fish oil into me.

I'm happy eating things like crisps and chips but again balanced out with other things. I used to be 'addicted' to Coca Cola. I was very proud of myself when I managed to stop drinking that and started Irn Bru instead but then I read the label and found out that it had caffeine in it as well! Later I moved onto Dr Pepper until eventually I began to accept that it was doing my teeth no good. I started drinking water instead. It was really boring at first but now I love it and drink loads.

Around that same time I started making smoothies. A bit of a palaver, soon I moved onto just fruit chopped up in yoghurt. Now I have that every day for my pudding (remember I'm Scottish). Fruit was always far too much of a bother to peel and eat so I never bothered but in my yoghurt it is delicious. I love trying all the different fruits and have a mixture of at least 2, such as strawberries and bananas and maybe blaeberries (the Scottish name). As they say fruit is naturally sweet, so I just use plain, very low fat, natural yoghurt. This all in all is a lovely healthy addition to my lifestyle. I used to love flavoured yoghurt, now I can't believe how sweet and sickly it tastes and I avoid it. If I have a cold I like to have a wee bit of honey in my yoghurt. It's funny Sue, my Step Mum doesn't like honey as she thinks it's too sweet but I don't really like sweet sugary things and I **love** honey.

I always have vegetables every day as well. School dinners with ice cream scoops of mashed turnip and home meals with a pile of plain boiled vegetables like leeks, plonked on the plate, really put me off a lot of veg. However I have found in the freedom of my own kitchen that veg can be cooked in many different ways and really is a nice treat.

I'm not one to go to the doctors or take medicine, although I will if it is really needed. A few years ago at a hospital check up, the Doctor was quite stunned at the thinness of my medical records. Our science teacher, Mr Cuthbert used to tell us that when you took pain killers for a headache it didn't actually stop the pain but just masked or killed the brain cells that were telling you that there was a pain. I have never taken much medicine since then. I have an, only slightly joking, theory that when people take medicine for a sore head, that it is the glass of water they take with it that actually cures the headache! He also told us that the effect of too much alcohol kills brain cells that never grow back. That didn't stop me drinking alcohol in my 'younger' days but I never really drink alcohol now. I was never that fussed unless I was out for a good night out, where, becoming drunk was all part of the fun. Now I just think of the horrible feeling of the next day. When it is just a single drink or so, I don't bother as I would much rather drink something that I enjoy the taste of more and feel that it is doing me good.

Mr Cuthbert also told us that chewing chewing gum gets your stomach ready to digest food and then when you don't swallow it your stomach starts the digestion process on itself and if you do swallow it you can't digest it and it just lies there. That put me off chewing gum for many years. I do however always have sugar free chewing gum after meals now as it cleans my teeth for me. I began to find that when I ate things like fruit and then later brushed my teeth that it was really sore. This shows a kind of typical Blanche twist on the 'normal' sensitive teeth problem. Most people get that from too hot or cold things, I get it from fruit!! The answer to this pain, for me, is to chew chewing gum straight after the food, perhaps the saliva washes the 'acid' away, I don't know but whatever happens, it works.

Mr Cuthbert was a good but scary and very strict teacher. I am very grateful to him for the day he ordered me to go to his study room for what I thought was going to be a terrible row. My friend Babs and I along with some others had been talking, carrying on and making jokes and running commentaries for quite some time in science. He ordered me to his room for a talk. It was absolutely terrifying. He had a fierce temper. But when I got there, he told me that I was a clever girl, that I was just wasting my time and that it was up to me whether I was going to start paying attention and getting on with my work or not. I really appreciated this praise and the way he didn't give me a row but left the decision up to me. So thank you Mr Cuthbert for your own idiosyncratic words of wisdom and scares which have stuck with me and some of your other pupils through the years. By the way I will always remember what idiosyncratic means as it is how a High School English teacher described my spelling.

So I'm a healthy, fit, active kind of person though not in a sporty kind of way. I hated some gym at school like cross-country and was always one of the last chosen for teams, which was horrible. With cross-country, I even used to come in after the ones who stopped for a smoke on the way round! Sports days were a complete torture and in later years a waste of a day. If I **had** to take part I did badly.

One year in the mid 1970s when we lived in Dollar, it was a Village Gala day. Being a 'Tom Boy', I was delighted, for the fancy dress parade, when I was dressed up in one of my big brothers Cub uniforms. A sign was made for me saying 'Woman's' Lib'. In those days, I don't think I had any idea what that really was. Well as the day went on I decided, at the last minute, that I wanted to take part in the sack race. Rushing to the start I took part in the race. At the finishing line an adult asked me, "Are you trying to prove a point Blanche?" It wasn't until later that it was explained to me that Dad had rushed me into the race not realising it had been a boys race!

Another story from that time is the embarrassment my family got when my Dad went down to parents night. Having just started seeing my, to be, Step Mum Sue, he wasn't expecting the whole village to be told about it with the gossip that followed my essay. Apparently I wrote how my Dad was now sleeping with a new lady who had ginger hair and was a vegetarian!

My years in Dollar were a brilliant time for me. We lived in a big house with a lovely interesting garden that led down to woods 'down the back'. I moved there when I was about 2 or 3 and left to come to Crieff at the very end of Primary Five. Not many years really but to me it was a lifetime. I **did not** want to leave.

The woods were a brilliant place to play. I spent many hours climbing trees, building dams, having picnics and making houses for fairies out of twigs, leaves and things.

Our lives were quite free then, or rather left to our own devices rather a lot. In those days us girls still dressed up in 'party frocks' for birthday parties. One day Dad got a phone call from someone asking why I wasn't at the party, he had forgotten all about it and rushed me down in my scruffy clothes. I remember really enjoying just being in my jeans when everyone else was all dressed up.

I remember walking down to school with Duncan and some others when someone asked what that stink was. It turned out to be the marmite from my breakfast that I still had all around my mouth. My Step Mum says that my lovely long hair was all tugs and tangles when she arrived. Apparently I only brushed over the surface never the underneath parts of my hair.

There was a really interesting cobbler in the Village called Mr Inch (I think). He had a 3 wheeler car and was in a wheel chair. Taken for shoes one day, I remember my Dad letting me buy boys black lace ups. In those days girls just didn't wear things like that. Mr Inch suggested some fancy laces to go with them, so I got long black and white laces as well. The laces were a bit embarrassing but I loved my shoes. There was always trouble later when taken to a shop to buy shoes, Dad and Sue never believed that I could tell that I didn't like any just by scanning round the shop as soon as I got in. I could though I could see the styles and knew that I didn't like them. (You know I always recently thought it was a new thing that I've really gone off shopping but maybe I had that trouble back then as well.)

I also started a liking for wearing hats, sometimes caps, but I did have one stripy woolly hat that I would wear everywhere, even to bed. My bed was full of cuddly toys, a great trick I found was that when Dads' friends came up to say goodnight to me, I would make them say good night to every cuddly toy as well, which managed to draw the process out for much longer until they got fed up. My Step Mum was reminding me the other day that I even had some stones in my bed.

Being a 'Tom Boy' when young, I wouldn't wear skirts. I was taken one time shopping and persuaded to buy denim culottes when I was told that they were a compromise, being more like jeans and shorts than a skirt. I only wore them once to school and was teased like mad and so never wore them again. A family friend also bought me a brown leathery corduroy type dress, during a series of Robin Hood on the telly, saying it was like a lady in Robin Hood's gang would wear. I believed her at first but again chickened out of actually wearing it. So although I definitely didn't want to come to Crieff, it did give me the chance to redesign myself and wear skirts without anyone laughing or knowing that it was odd.

But back to school sports. The last 2 years of High School I suddenly decided to just enjoy gym. I began to really enjoy it. We got some interesting things like badminton, squash and lacrosse. I even began to enjoy the team games more.

But I still, as an adult, am not a sports type kind of person. I did Tai Chi and Qigong for a while, which I loved. During the Qigong, I would go in my mind and visit a beautiful hilltop, mountain view, refreshing place. They changed the night and time of Tai Chi which didn't then suit my 'routines', so I left. I was going to carry on using a Tai Chi video. But it wasn't the same and I felt really stupid moving about like that in the flat, sure that the neighbours across the road would be wondering what on earth I was doing, so I stopped.

I think my routines are my way of looking after myself, but my friends tease me about it and my family worry. I like my meals at around the 'right' times. I don't like having my tea late. I don't mean in a precise, shoot the wife if it is not 6.00pm precisely kind of way but just in a general time of day kind of way. People think it's really weird that I make such a fuss about getting my lunch but to me it's important. Whether at home or work it is really important to me that I get my lunch, get away from the work area and eat a proper sitting down meal, without rushing. Again I believe that these things are very important for a healthy lifestyle. Mind you I absolutely hate if I am at a family meal and the meal is finished but everyone just sits there talking. I just want to get up and on and get other things done.

When a student, if a class was to go on at lunch time and I asked when we were going to have a break for lunch, people just stared at me, as they do, with that opened mouthed, silent amazement and then laughed.

I also love to have a bath early and then go to bed and read before I go to sleep. When there is a family doo or something that stops me having this routine I don't get to sleep for ages. No matter how tired I am, I just lie there while whole scenes and conversations play through my head like a video. It is very annoying and one of the reasons why I like to leave a thing nice and early but again that just makes my family worry and think that there is something 'wrong' with me.

I really wish that they wouldn't worry and would just accept me for who I am, a lovely, friendly, cheery person. Having said that it would be great to become much more flexible and enjoy socialising, doing different things and going places a lot more. That would be really good for me. I also realise that if I'm ever lucky enough to find my husband or have a family that of course my life and routines would have to change dramatically.

What family and friends don't seem to realise is that I know these things and would be happy to change in order to be able to have my **own** special person and family. They forget that I lived for many years in a crazy, largely male dominated household of many people as many as seven of us at one point. I can do it and I will when I have to. I suppose that is the same with me getting a job, only different in that I have **no** wish or longing to do that.

Part 2

My Career

So what career would I really love to have? I'd love to be an Art

Therapist. At least I think I would. Maybe I would just have no heart for

it once I got started.

Art Therapy would really suit me. It's often one to one work, which I do

best as it means I can really focus on that person and what we are doing.

I love Art. In this career people are working with Art but don't have to be

good at it. In fact being a good Artist may actually take away from the

whole healing process as people are thinking about what their work is like,

rather than just getting 'lost' in the whole process. Mind you the same

could happen with other non artists. I've met so many people who say,

'I'm no good at Art' and so believe that and don't have a go. This is where

Art Therapy will break down barriers. Teach people how to love the magic

of doing art, rather than worrying about the result and look of the finished

piece.

One time I was over at a neighbour's house drawing with the younger

than me kids. The wee boy said to his Dad (who was an artist) I think

Blanche is an even better artist than you Dad. His Dad answered that art is not about who is better or worse, good or bad but about enjoying the art. I loved that answer, it made a big impression on me and I have always remembered it.

I helped my Dad out at one of his 'Stone Fests', where I had a stall for people to paint stones. There was an article in their Drystone Walling magazine about the day. In it they mentioned my stall and myself, a lovely mention:

"Norman's daughter, Blanche, had everyone discovering their artistic side with her slate painting stand. A natural teacher, she coaxed the least likely people to have a go with some amazing results. In fact since that day I have heard several people say how they surprised themselves by having a go and how pleased they were with the results."
(Gazette, November 2006, (CSB))

That is why I'm so against rules and regulations in Art, including Art Literature. To me, Art shouldn't be about a stuffy or even a very trendy panel saying what is good, bad, what will/won't sell, what should/shouldn't be done. It should be about what you, yourself feel and love, what moves you personally **not** what the Jones' have.

I remember being in my brothers' room one day when the sun was shining in the window. I picked up a thin book called *Being There* by Jeremy Korsinski or something like that (It's Jerzy Kosinski, I was always extremely proud of myself being able to remember that name, which I can't usually do. Turns out I got it wrong(!!) not too bad though!). I read it all in one go (which is absolutely unheard of for me). I loved the book. It was about a man who got through everything and through his journey by letting people believe what they wanted to believe. People think that what other 'important people' say or do is right and what we should believe and so follow that view. This is a bit like The Emperors' New Clothes. I always try to use what I gained from that book, to make up my own mind and go by my own feelings.

I'd love to be a healer, which is also what Art Therapy is about. It's a kind of puzzle. A person brings themselves, takes part within the safety of the therapy room. The Art Therapist then facilitates the way for that person to carry out a journey. The process of that journey will affect that person and create learning and development in both the client and the therapist. It is a working through and out of the puzzle. I love doing puzzles.

So Art Therapy would really suit me but it would mean moving to

Edinburgh, spending more money that I don't have and it is really hard to get into. Maybe one day there will be many more opportunities, places and ways to study and become an Art Therapist. I do hope so and I do hope they hurry up. Did I tell you I'm already 38 (probably older by now!) (Yes 42 at this counting and it keeps flying on for some reason!) (Blooming heck I have been writing this book for a long time the count is now 47 years!)

So what would interest me? Well here are some recent thoughts on the subject:

Careers

Like	**Dislike**
Art	Phones
Creative	Rushing
Computers	Stuffiness
Data	Tight Deadlines
Learning	Bad Atmospheres
Education	Sales
Children	Falseness
Libraries	
Reading	
Proof Reading	
Nature	
Wildlife	**Extra Notes**
Plants	Need **Practical** Experience, Training
Therapies	Stay in Small Town,
Spiritual	Dependent on Bus, No Transport
Healing	
Design	
Helping People	

Working and Studying With:

Dyslexia

Autism (In Children)

Behaviour Problems

Research

Teaching

Archaeology

Archiving

Bookshop (Like Waterstones)

I've got a problem with moving away. Perhaps somewhat to do with my love life (a story for a whole other book) but also all the things I'm discussing and exploring in this book rolled into one. I tried to go away to University once when I was about 19, to do Architecture, I only lasted for the first term, up to Christmas. My Granny suggested I swap over to the Art College instead of coming back home. I've always regretted not taking her advice. Years later I had another go at leaving. I went down to start at Art College in Sunderland. From the first night, I got no sleep and was walking around in a trance like state, I couldn't think or cope and I only lasted a week.

Not long after I got back I went a night out with my friends' sister and ended up having to have a doctor called in for me. He thought I might have taken drugs, a most definite no no in my life. So I went to see my own Doctor in the next few days and it was decided that I had had a panic attack. Deciding never ever to have one of those again, I started going to see a Person Centred Therapist for Counselling. I really enjoyed that and felt that it got me moving again.

Not long after that I even managed to apply for and get a job. It was a one week work trial at a brilliant place where people could come in and paint their own pottery mugs, plates, ornaments etc. There was also play fun and making beads etc for the kids. Unfortunately the lady owner was totally 'mad' and for me very confusing. I tried my best but only lasted the week. It really shook my confidence in the job department again and set me back a huge, huge way. I will talk about this whole experience in more detail later.

But anyway, back to the career ideas. I find when I say things like, 'I'd love to do Archaeology' to people at the Job Centre or Job Club, that they just say "oh yes", are quiet for a minute and then go back to searching, for me, for 'ordinary' jobs!

Archaeology sounds like a brilliant career. I love puzzles, working things out, searching for things, paying attention to details, working outdoors but also indoors, drawing, using computers, finding out things, learning, searching for data, collecting, sorting and collating things. So again it would seem the ideal career for me.

I remember at school, in Guidance, searching through the ancient, very sparse, 'Sign Posts' careers box. I always looked at the Archaeology card and thought that it sounded brilliant. But the card said that you needed Latin. I was in the second class for English, only the top class got Latin and so I thought that I couldn't do Archaeology.

Another idea that I had was Architecture. I remember suggesting it in a careers interview at school. The person suggested an Archaeological Technician instead. I asked why not an Architect and was told that that was much harder to get into. So being the stubborn, determined bugger that I am, when it comes to some things, I ended up going to do Architecture. This, as you know, only lasted one term! (Can I just mention here that I got my Dad to read this book, which was quite a scary thing to do. Actually he really enjoyed it which I was really pleased about. He did mention though about the word "bugger" saying it was really rude. I agree with him, I don't swear much and probably a lot less than I used to but I am leaving in this language which appears here and in my diary pages later as it was what I said at the time and also obviously wasn't meant in any literal manner! Apologies here to anyone who is sensitive to such matters.)

So back to Archaeology, again money is needed and being prepared to move away. The way to get into it, is a degree which I can't afford and moving away to do it which again I can't afford and am not brave enough to do. I would move away if I had my true love to move with me.

Another way in is to **pay** to go and do voluntary work. Before you do this you need some experience at local British digs. Something I would need a car for. I told the job centre that they would be much better giving me driving lessons than sending me to the Job Club. Strangely they didn't take me up on the offer!

Perhaps again the stuffiness, rules and regulations of Archaeology wouldn't suit me anyway. I just want to find treasures. I have recurring dreams about finding clean, whole treasures and gems in the earth, sand, stones and even under the sea. I love those dreams. I would really love to go to Egypt and see and feel the atmosphere of the pyramids and visit the big museum. In fact I **will** definitely do that.

See how my head jumps. That bit about Egypt, seemed to come from nowhere, but at the time of writing fitted into my flow of thoughts. You see when I was at Uni doing Architecture, one of our Lecture subjects was actually Archaeology, Egyptian, while I was there and all those thoughts brought that memory back to the surface.

What jobs have I done? When we first came to this town, in 1978, Dad bought a small shop and turned it into a craft shop. I often helped out there, often sole charge, which wasn't bad for a young teenager. The shop was across the road from what was then William Lows, the supermarket or "Willie Lows" as we called it.

We moved to Crieff in 1978, so I would have been 10. For our first year, we rented a big house. It had a locked room up the stairs. Obviously that room would have been full of the owners' belongings. At the time it drove me mad with curiosity and thoughts of magic rooms, treasures and gateways to other worlds. All I could see through the keyhole was some vague shapes and rays of dusty sunlight shining in at times.

One day I was so excited as I had asked if I could make the meal and was allowed to. I was really to regret this later. Dad got home to announce that he and Sue had discussed it and decided that us kids (Duncan, Christopher and I) would now make the meal one day a week each. This was actually brilliant training for adult life. But within a few years, added with the ever growing list of Saturday cleaning day jobs, it became a real drag.

(Now that last paragraph was a real jump from nowhere but you see I was thinking of Ogilvie Bank the big house that we rented for a year and that was where that making the tea thing happened. So the memory obviously just jumped into my head because of thinking about the house.)

Another brilliant but hard life lesson was how making the meal worked. We were given a certain amount of money. I think it was only a couple of pounds in those days. With that, we had to plan and buy the food for a meal for us all, including pudding and a vegetarian choice for Sue.

Back to 'Willie Lows', (see my head did have a reason for mentioning it earlier!!) which luckily was, just across from the shop. Quite a few times, I would have that horrible dread and loss of blood in my head, then thumping heart and blushing feeling of not having enough money. I would have to leave my shopping at the cheque out and rush over to the shop to ask Dad for more money. These lessons taught me how to buy nice things but also be really careful with money. It was usually a caramel sponge cake (my favourite, that I couldn't resist but it was expensive) that would let me down and put the price too high.

When we had Mr Kippling cakes, the last one was always split into 5, later 6 pieces. No one ever said "oh you can have my bit".

My wee brother Findlay was born in 1980, the summer between my ending Primary 7 and going to High School. That summer we moved to our new house, where Dad and Sue still live today.

I remember being mortally embarrassed when Dad started pushing things down the hill to our new house, manually, in something with wheels. I can't remember if it was the small car trailer or the wheelbarrow.

Dads' wheelbarrows still embarrassed my wee brothers and me many years later when he would drive to his dyking jobs with his wheelbarrow fixed to the top of the car wheel up. Don't ask me why this is so embarrassing but I can assure you that it is!

From then on my role as babysitter started. I looked after Findlay and later Calum, often (at least a couple of evenings every single week) as they grew up and also did babysitting jobs for friends and neighbours.

I eventually had to stop babysitting for families with cats, as I would be fine when the parents left but by the time they arrived back I had "devil eyes" and a red, streaming nose, which is how I found out about my cat allergy.

I was always a 'snotty' kid but don't remember thinking much about it. I know my Granny used to say I was all blocked up (nose ways) because I'd been lying on the carpet cuddling Beth (our Old English Sheep Dog). I didn't care. I loved Beth. She was my friend through thick and thin.

So it turned out that I 'babysat' for over 2 decades. It's funny how employers don't seem in the slightest bit interested in babysitting as work experience. Being a parent, I would have thought, should be an excellent example of experience for people applying for jobs but seems to me, to be largely ignored. In fact 'Mothers' years out seem to be seen as a break from work rather than an incredibly hard, wide and varied work experience.

Not long after we moved to the new house, I got my first proper, paid job, looking after a young toddler, while his Mum gave piano lessons. Young and inexperienced in life as I was, this job taught me a lesson I'll never forget. In childcare, you are the calm, responsible, adult and they are the kid! The boy and I were having fun playing with his toys, when he decided to grab and pull a handful of my hair. Finding this very sore and annoying, I decided, in my great wisdom to teach him a lesson and pulled his hair back. Unsurprisingly he started screaming. I calmed him down and got on with playing.

When his Mum came through later, she asked what all the noise had been about. Being an honest person, I couldn't lie and so told her, getting more embarrassed as I went on, how "he'd pulled my hair, so . . . "

"You pulled it back," she finished for me. "Yes", I agreed. Strangely enough, I was never asked back after that. Just as well it wasn't nowadays when you get put in prison for just looking at a child!

(Don't panic, I, in no way, agree with hitting or hurting children or anything else come to that. I was just having a discussion today about how much society and our views have changed on that matter. I grew up with the belt at school and smacks at home being normal and perfectly acceptable. I never got the belt although the whole class was threatened with it once. I only got a real smack as in getting put over the knee once and that is when I ate the whole of the Cash and Carry box of ice poles. I used to think that a short sharp shock as in a wee slap might teach a child not to do something but my philosophy now would be, I hope, that it is wrong to teach a child to respond to anything with violence of course communication is the answer. This is perhaps a much longer way of teaching and learning but hopefully a much more positive way.)

I never made that much money babysitting, although it seemed a lot at the time. I remember hearing a few years later that my 'perfect' cousin got £5 an hour babysitting. That made me so jealous as I thought how rich I would have been over the years if I'd got that much.

My family didn't pay me for babysitting although Sue did once offer me Driving Lessons, to say thank you. I declined as is my annoying way when someone first offers or suggests a change to me. Now, with driving lessons costing an absolute fortune, I really wish I had taken her up on the offer.

(I always seem to have to say no to something when first asked as it is a change to my routine or ways and I don't like changes but then when I think about it I often decide it might be ok. Dad now tells everyone 'oh that will be Blanche', when he has phoned me for something and I have said no. He knows that I really just need time to think about it.)

I did one time start to learn to drive. I was driving along quite happily, it's quite easy just putting your foot on the accelerator and steering. But then Dad told me to "pull in there", pointing to lay-by, just before a small nearby village. I panicked, I knew I had to move down gears but how was I supposed to do that and pull in all at once, right now? Dad calmly said, "never mind just keep on going through the village", so I did.

However it is very deceptive when you are learning, how fast you are actually going, especially, as I now was, nervous. I didn't realise that I was going too fast until a lot of car horns started peeping. I went round the nasty blind bend ending up on the wrong side of the road with a car coming towards us.

Dad calmly leaned over, took the wheel and steered us into the side. He then drove us home!

Not long after that my friend Paul, his brother and another friend all decided to go to the cinema. We were running a bit late and Paul being a young man who, as they do, believed he was invincible, decided to get us there quickly.

There were a few cars in a row, not thinking about why they were in a row, he decided to overtake them and get on at top speed. Unfortunately we 'met' the reason that they were stopping, a car that was turning off to the right.

He swerved to avoid the car, which we did hit. We ended up in the siding. Our spectacular crash blocked the road both ways for half an hour. During which time, I sat and held Paul, whose blood I ended up covered in.

The car had to be cut up to get Paul out. Strangely enough apart from some soreness, bumps and Paul's' many stitches, we were all fine physically.

Very shaken up from that experience, I took a couple of days off work. The day I decided to go back, I went up to the bus station to catch my bus to Auchterarder. Unfortunately our driver decided to be a hero and try to catch the Perth bus (the opposite direction to our actual bus route) that a lady had just missed. We all, in our big bus, went tearing out the very same road that the crash had happened, at a ridiculous speed. He soon gave up and turned back but it had definitely not helped my already very fragile state of mind.

After that I never went back to driving lessons. This is a real setback now as I would love to learn but I can't even afford the lessons never mind the test, then a car!

(Now that I am working again and have a good wage I know it is time for me to learn to drive and get a wee car. I will but it is very scary and is much easier just to put off. Further note to this with extra years added on: I have lost my full time job due to job cuts and only work 3 days a week now. This has put me back to not being able to afford even lessons never mind anything more and I'm still not able to drive.)

There seems to be a very, very suspicious high number of people who fail their tests nowadays, passing third time seems to be about normal round here at the moment. I do hope that no one is trying to make extra money out of us poor learner drivers.

It seems just about every job I look at now, says driving licence **essential** as one of its criteria. I think that this is funny in nanny jobs. I would love to say to them, "your kids should be walking, it's good for them!" I wouldn't get the chance though as it seems impossible to get past the check point barrier of agencies to actually talk to the parents.

These check points of desirable and essential attributes must rule out so many capable people these days. It's lost its thought and flexibility. Having to have an extremely basic practical childcare qualification is another example, never mind if you have a degree in Child and Youth Studies and have looked after children of all ages for nearly 3 decades!

When I was in High School, it seemed like **everyone** except me and Fiona Johnstone (hello to you Fiona) worked at Willie Lows, the supermarket in the Square that I was telling you about earlier. I had no interest in working there but I did get quite jealous of the clique that it built up and I loved to hear my best friend Babs' stories of the fun and nonsense that they all got up to.

Later Sue's Mum, Iris, got me a Saturday job cleaning chalets. It was funny years later as my brother, now quite well to do, in a living and working in England or abroad rather than Scotland kind of way, started to take his families' summer holidays at those very same Chalets.

But back then I never thought I would be on the guest side of things. I enjoyed my work at the Chalets. The 'wifies' were mostly all lovely and looked after me. One, Mary Dow, would give me tips like shining the taps with a dry towel to make things look extra sparkly and clean, which I still do when cleaning my own bathroom and it looks lovely.

There were 3 Mary's, Dow, Thomson and Noble, all lovely friendly ladies. I still have a good blether with Mary Dow nowadays when I meet her on the bus.

The owner also cleaned with us, which I liked, all mucking in together. I learned to count Chalets yet to be done, rather than hours, which made the day go much faster. I used to sing away as I was cleaning. It was at the Chalets when I discovered my dust allergy, after a hand hoover fell apart showering me in lots of smelly old dust.

We had great fun there. I get terrible frights and remember one time when I was cleaning a bathroom. One of the ladies came in and spoke to me. I was 'lost' in what I was doing and got such a fright that I screamed, jumped up and fell over landing in the bath, much to all of our hilarity.

Having had lots of home Saturday cleaning practice and with the ladies help and advice, I became good at my job. I was praised and soon promoted to sometimes being allowed to clean kitchens! One Summer I also got a few weekends work showing prospective buyers round the new time share chalets. The then owners, Mr and Mrs Colquhoun still say a nice hello to me when I see them in the street.

I was a waitress for a few months, full time. It was really hard, tiring work. We weren't ever allowed to do nothing, folding napkins was the fill in if we ever really did get a gap. The job was mind numbing and drove me to College, where I studied and managed to get myself through an HND (Higher National Diploma) in Computing. That was in the days when everything you did on a computer had to be keyed in by words. There was no mouse, no menus, no pictures, no nothing, or should I say no anything?!

Following on from that qualification, I managed to get myself a job as a Production Controller at a factory in Auchterarder. My Step Mum noticed the advert and encouraged me to apply. My Computing teacher advised me against the place, saying he had heard bad things about it. I just gave him a row and told him not to spoil it. I was so proud of getting the job.

I had to get up really early to catch the bus, work all day in the works office which had no windows then catch the bus home again.

At some times of the year, I didn't see daylight (one of the worst tortures a person could give me). I remember looking over at the hills on my way down the road to the factory in the morning and praying that a UFO would come and take me away!

The boss' son was quite nice but then he would go in terrible tempers or tantrums really I suppose and throw things about. I remember a really loud crash when he threw one of the huge industrial sized spanners at a machine.

The place was covered in a red sawdust from the box making. The factory made wooden veneer boxes or drums and table mats. It was long before the fuss we have now of Health and Safety and no smoking policies. Everyone smoked, apart from me. At the canteen I would sit at a metre square table with people on all sides smoking their cigarettes. They were all very cliquey, it took me the full 2, nearly 3, years that I was there before I finally managed to get them all worked out and be slightly accepted.

In the end the works manager and the head of one department had a wee word with me and warned me that the bosses were planning to get rid of either me or one of the girls from the front office. So taking this kick up the bum, that I always need, I applied for a job at Perth College. I didn't get it but a few months later they phoned me and said they were so impressed with me at the interview that they wondered if I would like a new job that had come up. Things like that could happen in those days. While the way jobs vacancies are dealt with nowadays is supposed to be so much fairer I certainly did not find it fair to go for jobs that the company already had an idea who they wanted and just advertised the job because they had to by law. At least now the Council jobs say "internal only" if they are doing that but that in itself was extremely frustrating, to find out about a job vacancy that you weren't even allowed to apply for, why on earth tell us in the first place?

While still working at the factory I had really hated the thought of getting out of bed in the morning. Tom who owned my flat was so worried about me he phoned my friend, Babs to have a word. I was sleep walking and mumbling in my sleep.

One of the factory workers was off with depression. I tried having a word with my doctor but he just said well take an aspirin before you get up. I'm not a complainer and I reckon a cheery person, saying I get bad headaches in the morning probably just wasn't the same as the sob stories that Doctors are used to!

So luckily eventually I was saved and started my new job as a Desk Top Publisher at Perth College. Now that job was perfect, I absolutely loved it. I had to learn how to use a mouse as at my old work we just used spreadsheets and the keyboard to create forms, calendars etc. It's difficult now to imagine not using a mouse but I remember struggling at the interview where we had a practical test. As soon as I moved the mouse the cursor would go flying off the screen and I couldn't find it again. (I suppose now there are many people who don't use a mouse again as it is all touch screen type things, I am not up to date at all in that department, not even having a mobile phone.)

I soon got into my new job. Getting paid for sitting all day being creative and using computers to make modules, leaflets etc was brilliant. I got on great with the staff and soon they were coming to me when they were stuck with computing problems.

Every now and again, I would get really tired and just not be able to cope with getting up in the morning. Now I've learned that I just get a lot more tired for a few days around period time but I hadn't worked that out in those days. Also I really do need a good night sleep even just the slightest bit of interrupted sleep and I can't 'think straight'. In those days I hadn't quite worked out that the trick was to go to bed at a good early time and get a full night sleep. So sometimes when I was really tired in the morning and needed to go back to sleep, I would skive off.

The lovely ladies (Helen and Dolores) in the office, who I am still friends with, weren't stupid. Eventually Helen would say to me we'd prefer if you came in late than lie to us about being ill. So every now and again I would come in late, the result a perfect attendance record.

I don't actually get ill much at all. My doctors' records must be one of the smallest folders there is. I used to love getting full attendance on my report cards at school. (The doctors' folder will have grown now sadly as I had to go to hospital for major surgery to get a "monster" 15cm cyst along with my left ovary and fallopian tube removed in 2011. I always remember what year it was because that same year I had my bedroom decorated and the magical date was 11/11/11, which we wrote on the bare walls.)

Perhaps that (never going to the doctors and loving getting full attendance reports that is, for those of you who might have lost the thread!!) all happened because our P1 (P1 means primary one, in Scotland we have Primary 1 to 7 then 1st to 4th year High School with optional 5th to 6th year. Nowadays they also put the kids to pre-school so they are stuck into society and being trapped earlier and earlier) teacher would give us all a lollipop if we had all been there the whole week. Funnily enough it was a 'drumstick' which I don't actually like and always gave to my brothers. But anyway it just shows what a positive long term effect rewards may have on a person.

Talking of giving sweeties to my brothers, I don't like chocolate and never have as long as I can remember. My cousin got me to try it once at my Granny's but I spat it out in the sink straight away! I do however actually remember eating chocolate mint yoyos at one time. There is also a story of me at Edinburgh Zoo. Granny and Grampa Roberts had taken me for a great day at the zoo. On the way home Grampa asked me what was the best thing about the day, 'the smarties' I answered! So I must have eaten them at one time as well. Actually recently I reminded someone in the family about that story and my big brothers and I all disagreed about who was the person in the story eating the smarties. I believe it was me because I can remember Granny telling me the story but then maybe I have it mixed up as it was just a story telling rather than me remembering the actual scene in my head. Once I hear a story, I make that scene in my head and remember it from there. So that truth can be different from when I actually live a scene and remember it in my head.

But anyway I don't like chocolate and never have. There is a family story from when I was a baby. My Mum had made a chocolate birthday cake for David Lochhead the oldest son of some family friends. Apparently they came through and found me. I had knocked the cake down and eaten the whole thing! I have no recollection of that whatsoever.

So Easter and Easter Eggs was a very boring, unfair, time for me. If I did ever get chocolate from someone, I would take great pleasure in rationing it out to my brothers as long as they were nice to me!!

So back to school. I remember Miss Gay(!) my primary 1 teacher as being an old, very strict lady. I have a memory of being taken out of school dinners and stood in the corner because I hadn't written straight on the lines.

Those school dinners, at Strathdevon Primary were absolutely horrible and a huge torture in my life. Being really fussy, meal times generally tended to be a bit of nightmare in my childhood with many horrible memories of struggles and rows connected with food and adults inability to understand the horror and complete impossibility of eating a food which one doesn't like!

But the school dinners were a million times worse. There were ice cream scoops of mashed tatties and mashed turnips, revolting puddings like semolina (semi-slimy) with prunes in it aaaaaaaaaaaaaagh etc etc. I still don't like anyone mashing my potatoes unless it is me and they are on my plate. I also can't stand any puddings such as rice pudding, custard etc.

Two other clear images I get from that canteen and general school hall are one of a boy who was only there for a very short time. He was foreign perhaps Native American? I remember being fascinated when he showed us that he could bend all his fingers at the top phalange without bending them in the middle.

The other memory of that hall is us all dancing around in our green gym pants, that had a wee pocket in them, with our black plimsolls, that I kept in a blue draw string bag. We were swaying around the hall doing what was called 'music and movement' and pretending to be trees.

I tell you these wee stories of my memories so that you can see the kind of really strong snapshot type memories I have of certain strange things. The other year there was a whole load of family and friends all crammed around a big round table in a café in Auchterarder. A while after that meal I asked some of the people that had been there to sketch the table and place everyone that had been there and where they sat. It was really interesting. I knew exactly where everyone had been with no question of whether I was wrong. Dad, my brother Chris and my nephew Jack got some of it right but it was really interesting to see how what was important to them affected their memory of the scene. For instance Dad remembered the American lady next to him and Jack and Chris each remembered themselves next to each other even though neither of those things was right. None of them knew which individual baby twin sat where just the area that they were in, nor which way round the twins parents were. I wasn't at all interested in and didn't try to remember that scene but it was completely clear in my head. Perhaps because I sat and watched and listened a lot where as other people talk more?

Yet there is no way I could answer you questions on names, dates etc of things that I learned off by heart for exams in school and College. Not even say about a week after I had sat the exams. I remember doing really well in an Art History exam. While in the exam, I was having trouble remembering the names, dates etc, so I decided just to focus on describing the paintings as I could see them really easy in my head. I was really pleasantly surprised when this ended up in really good marks.

So back to my DTP job, which I loved. I even coped fine when they moved us from the Open Learning Office into the Open Access room next door. There was a connecting door so it wasn't too much of a change for me to cope with. I got to know loads of the staff and got a run home in the car with Helen and my friend Babs' husband Graham. Their friendship helped me cope with going to some of the end of term nights outs etc, as I knew I had people to look after me and a lift home from Perth.

I still wasn't the most social of people and would do things like go to the College library and read at lunch times. My idea of heaven WASN'T going to the staffroom and talking to everyone. It was a large busy staffroom in those days.

I lasted a number of years at Perth College. It was a good pay and I enjoyed myself, the job and the laughs, the acceptance and understanding of my funny wee ways. Helen would always introduce me to people by saying, 'this is Blanche she is very strange but we love her!' They would tease me at lunch time when I always laid my tray out ready for lunch each time in exactly the same way with my bit of chewing gum, juice etc.

Then we got a new Principle. I remember thinking he was great and handsome. But he was actually a small man with not much 'heart' as far as I could see. Isn't funny how the glamour of a big boss works for a while. It's the same with people playing in a band on stage. They seem lovely and fanciable but I bet they wouldn't be the slightest bit interesting in the light of day down among us mere mortals! But back to the College and the new principle, things started to change. Open Learning, my base of support that worked so well, started being changed and split up. We, the DTP people, were moved to another floor, joined with others and made into a DTP department.

We were given a new boss. I remember, at one of the evaluation one-to-one meetings I had with her, she suggested I go for a job in graphics. I took this as a very discouraging thing believing that she didn't appreciate me or understand my worth. Thinking about it, that was probably actually my fault. A while before that my friend and work colleague, Angela, and I had both gone for our same job but with supervisor responsibility. Angela got the job and afterwards they told me that it had been a very close thing. They had chosen Angela as she had been talking about what she wanted to do in the future whereas I had said that I was happy to be doing what I was doing now. I'd remembered that so when my new boss started asking me what I could see myself doing in the future, I had started telling her, which was probably not quite how their original advice had been meant. But I didn't remember or think of that at the time when the new boss started suggesting jobs that I might prefer. I just thought she doesn't want me.

Then she started us having to fill in time sheets, this really angered me. Back at the factory I had been in charge of timesheets and clock cards and now here I was being asked to fill one in. It took away my sense of freedom and made me feel untrusted and unvalued. I also didn't like lying if I wanted too go a wee walk for a break or do a bit of my own work. It just made it feel more and more like a 9-5 day in day out prison sentence to me.

One of the other DTPers was leaving to go travelling round the world. I was so jealous of this, it was the kind of escape I longed for and dreamed about but there was no way I would be brave enough to do that. However my Granny (the best Granny in the world) had died the year before and left me a load of money.

The first thing I did was brave up my courage and go on a cruise. I chose a wee Cruise Ship, The Black Prince, so that I wouldn't have to face all the crowds and glitz of the bigger ships. We went to Madeira, The Canary Islands, Tangiers and Lisbon. I loved it, I was safe and got to go on small organised tours in each place and see the world in a safe, magical, luxurious way.

I loved Madeira the best but I think that was because I hadn't seen land for a number of days (must have been how the old sailors felt!).

The Cruise ships are huge and have stabilisers so we are spoilt. The only bit where I felt the slightest seasick was when we were going through the Bay of Biscay. My Uncle John, a keen sailor, had warned me about the Bay of Biscay, but it was absolutely fine on the way down, it was on the way back that it got wild. I was doing fine just sitting looking out the window when another passenger came up to talk to me. Unfortunately he stank of sweat. I have an extremely sensitive sense of smell. I hate to think what I would be like if I ever got pregnant when all expectant mothers seem to get ill really easily from smells. I quickly had to excuse myself and run to my cabin. I lay on the cold shower room floor and eventually felt better without ever actually being sick, thank goodness.

Did I tell you my Dad has no sense of smell? He was born like that, it's called anosmia. It must be quite rare as I never hear of other people with it. A few people say 'oh I've got a terrible sense of smell as well', which annoys me as it isn't the same at all. Apparently his Mum, my Granny Haddow, never believed him and always used to say "oh yes my father used to say that as well". That's according to my Dad anyway. I never know how distorted or true his stories of his Mum and Dad and their characters are. Not that Dad would consciously lie, like me he never (as never as one can get in life anyway) tells lies, which perhaps isn't always a good thing.

(I have met someone else now who actually has no sense of smell. My sister in laws family friend Marrion had an accident and lost her sense of smell. I think that is the story but it may have been distorted in memory of the telling of it. She worked with perfume which obviously then turned out to be not so handy after that! That is still not the same as being born with no sense of smell though. Imagine if you had never known smell and then you suddenly could, I wonder if you would go around being sick everywhere?)

We (Dad and I) have come to think that Dad's Mum, Granny Haddow, definitely had a lot of the 'troubles' peculiarities that we see in us and Jack, my nephew, who is on the autistic spectrum.

So Dad can't smell which may, at times, have its advantages! He is the best person I know at cleaning up sick! Although he does point out that he still hates doing that job. It could also be dangerous in not being able to smell gas etc. In recent years there was a worrying incident when Dad, sitting at the computer in the dining room, forgot that he had left a pot on the cooker which burned dry. The smoke alarm, in the hall, eventually went off but of course we would have all smelt it long before that whereas Dad had no idea at all.

Growing up we learnt to avoid saying we smelt something, as Dad would ask us to track down the smell. He just didn't or couldn't believe that this was a very hard thing to do and humans just can't work like dogs do with smell.

I think that way of growing up has made my sense of smell hyper sensitive. I always get paranoid about things like gas smells when no one else seems to be able to smell them. My brother Duncan says the same. He found a gas leek in his house long before anyone else could even smell it.

Dad always moans about tasteless food, not enough salt in cooking, the 'horrible' texture of pasta etc. It was only in recent years that I actually began to realise that his opinion of other peoples cooking just isn't a fair one. He loves vinegary things pickles, chocolate gingers etc. It's obvious that textures are much more important to him in food and that he can't tell a lot of difference between some flavours. Having said that he is very good at telling when something needs more or less salt and things like that. I never know that I have had too much salt in a meal until that night when I go to bed and wake up in the night with a mouth like a desert and usually bad dreams to go with it.

Both my big brothers are colour blind. They are actually 'red/green' colour blind. I used to love helping them with their felt tip choosing. I really loved having the huge long packets of felt tips and organising them into order by colour ranges. In fact I still do love doing that.

The colours they actually can't see a difference between, I fount out over the years, are particular shades of pink and grey and also between green and brown colours. I can still picture and show you the colours that they would have trouble with. I do this by picturing the old felt tips that they used to get mixed up and using those colours in my memory to look for those particular colours in life.

So back to my cruise! It was a great experience and I am really glad that I was brave enough to do it. Thank you Granny Roberts.

It wasn't all plain sailing! It wasn't the best thing being on my own. I couldn't have a long lie, as the cleaning lady would come in at a certain time. There was no lock on the cabin door. One day she came in when I was getting dressed. She went out again showing me the 'do not disturb' sign as she went.

The trouble was I would have had to wake up early to hang the sign out before I had my long lie.

I can't get back to sleep once I am up and about in the morning. If I want to go to the loo and then get back to sleep I have to go slowly, periodically opening and closing alternate eyes and not putting any lights on nor talking to anyone.

It takes me a really long time to get to sleep. My Dad has a wonderful talent of being able to sleep anywhere, straight away and wake up a few minutes later greatly refreshed. He does this if he needs to when on a long car journey, just stops the car and is right as rain in a few minutes or so. That's a strange saying isn't it, 'right as rain'?

I've seen Dad sleep soundly on the sitting room floor with kids jumping over him. But I definitely CAN'T do that and so like and very much need a long, quiet, relaxing sleep.

That wouldn't work obviously if I got up to hang the 'do not disturb' sign out in the morning, so I tried to hang it out at night as I went to bed. It only lasted about one night and then disappeared. I don't know if it was the cleaner fed up with it or another passenger that pinched it! My life is full of such strange problems that just don't seem to happen to 'normal' people or maybe just aren't important to them.

With the ship being small the passengers were mostly old and 'posh'. I have always looked young to the point of getting annoyed when yet another person referred to me as a 'girl' no matter how old I was. Now I've got some white hairs and despairing (as only a lady can) at moving

92

into my 40s, I don't mind people thinking I look young anymore. In fact I'm beginning to wonder if I don't look young anymore as I look in the mirror at my laughter lines and white hairs. I think you have to be close up though, as people still seem to think of me as just a silly wee girl. Perhaps it doesn't help that I am most definitely not a lady to wear makeup or dye my hair. (Now it is getting nearer to 50 and I am, I think, beginning to look like a "wifie", recently I have been looking at certain photos of myself and thinking I look older but then I am!)

By the way, I say white hairs as I hate when people say 'grey hairs' they are not grey, they are white. I also hate when people say 'red' hair instead of ginger. It's not red, if anything, it is orange but people don't say that. (Now by the way that my hair is going more grey I am leaning more towards saying grey hairs as that is what they look like as a whole now, it is funny (interesting) to read and see how I am growing, maturing and ageing during the process of writing this book.)

Anyway, so a lot of the people on the cruise thought I was awful young. Mind you I was young to be on a cruise on my own without a rich husband to pay my way.

Some of the people were lovely. I was placed for my meals at a table with a threesome, a sister, brother and his wife. One of them was called Vi. I can't remember the others names, they lived on the Isle of Wight. They really made me feel welcome.

I'd like to thank them. Apparently they phoned my Dads after the cruise to check that I got home safely which was really nice of them. I hate giving anyone my phone number. Probably subconsciously because I hate the intrusion in my life and the control it gives over to them, I don't know? I also really hate waiting for the phone to ring, so make a fuss and try to avoid at all costs, when someone says they will phone me back. I'm getting a wee bit better with phones now and can even make some important calls but don't tell anyone!

So I'd like to thank Vi oh and I think it was Val and the man for looking after me. I found their address that I had lost at the time, many years later when cleaning out a drawer and really wanted to send them a Christmas card but I was always worried in case one of them might have died or something by then and I didn't want to upset them.

But some of the people were a bit more annoying and not so nice. I always longed to get a job on a cruise ship in later years but actually, I bet I would have hated it. I reckon it would have felt like a prison and I would have hated the falseness of being polite to all those idiots.

I wrote a bit of a diary when on the cruise:

No way out, trapped, surrounded by a black moving landscape, no wildlife, nothing except the odd plank of wood! I wonder how long and how far that has travelled? . . .

(That reminds me of the song 'I joined the navy to see the world and what did I see? I saw the sea!')

. . . As for in here, nothing but happy, boring old couples. As one 74 year old Welsh man told me, "they are all geriatrics".

The highlight of my day, a bingo game for 'singles'. Only 4 of us turned up, so we had to resort to allowing another 2 couples, bloodthirsty at the chance of winning a bottle of champagne, to join us.

It is actually brilliant here, nothing to do, no one to tell me what or when to do anything. I wish the boring, set in their ways old buggers would stop looking at me as if I was one of the servants or even worse just an odd out of place 'thing' that doesn't belong.

"Why on earth did you do that?" said one of the not quite so old, old snobs. Talking about myself coming on holiday on my own, she couldn't believe that I would do that. The fact that she was doing the same didn't come into it. I suppose she had once been married and now a widower and so it was acceptable or perhaps it was just because she was an old Madame and I am a young Miss.

They all must think I have been sent here by my strict Aunt to repent my sins and find myself a rich, suitable 'young' bachelor. Fat bloody chance. I have spotted lets say only 3 men who come anywhere near having any looks left. . . .

(Oooh I really was one of those nasty, selfish, youths then wasn't I!!)

. . . One who has his arm attached to his rather bedraggled, worn, lady friend. Another who has an adoring wife, a mad auntie looking lady who seems to have attached herself to the family but ought to be related and a beautiful wee boy whom they don't really seem to know how to deal with, although he behaves extremely well.

The third man the only good looking one has very glazed, grey eyes, a

very rough, tough looking wife, a spoilt bratty looking little girl and a
beautiful wee baby boy, yet to be spoilt by his suspicious looking family.

I reckon either he hits her and hides behind his quiet good looks, with her
having earned her tough looking air. Or she hits him with her tough,
bullying, looking way and he cowers quietly showing nothing behind his
grey glazed eyes.

Anyway it is getting cold sitting here. I am going to try not changing for
dinner, I wonder if I should, if I will get away with it? I am too scared to
go exploring, to barge in anywhere, I wish I had someone with me,
someone to give me strength, so I could act my air of not caring, of being
loud and brutish.

Why can't I be like that on my own, why do I have to be so shy?
Everyone is meant to act, everyone is apparently nervous but they all put
on an act. Or in the case of these people here, the timid wee wife hides
behind her loud pompous husband or in some cases the other way round.
It makes you sick, their single beds, their loud views, their 'I'm better than
you' walk. I hate them they are all boring, old farts.

My my, I am bitter. I must be fed up and lonely, I wish I could just be alone, but I can't see the sea from my cabin. I love the sea. It is so beautiful, dark, deep and terrifying. Never mind your cheep fun fair thrills, or horror videos, give me the sea and its hidden creatures and landscapes anytime. The deep, dark, unknown but beautiful and intriguing sea. My life before this one, it must have been living and working from the ocean.

It's cold here now I think I'll move on. Perhaps the posh lounge where the Casino is. I bet I chicken out and retreat, like an old hermit crab, back to my cabin and safety!

Well, I made it here. Don't think I'll stay though, what if someone reads over my shoulder. Maybe they will think that I'm a great novelist and start talking to me. I hope not, I've gone into the depressive stage where I don't want anyone to talk to me, to cheer me up. I suppose I have to and face those 3 at dinner. A sister, brother and his wife. They all share a cabin together, all have the same views, won't do anything without each other. I wonder if they have mad passionate sex together?

The sister met me for the singles bingo today. She sat very seriously and won the champagne and would have won the other prize too, if the girl hadn't messed up calling out the numbers.

I've moved now, I've found a seat, bright, by the window and a frightfully, frightfully couple sitting behind me. He doesn't like the "terrible music". I hadn't noticed whether the music was terrible or not. Never mind they have settled down to the newspaper. Oh now they have started up again. She doesn't know what to do, ho ho ho oh rather. Can't eves drop any longer she talks too low. Oh I think they are doing the ships' quiz, oh "it's so easy". I looked at that earlier and couldn't answer a thing. Oh foods awful, that is "ofool" not awful! Well this is getting pretty boring. I'm not surprised they all sleep alone, they must get bored to death of each other. Oh here, now he is off. I reckon I'll be off too. Och I don't know, what am I supposed to do?

I'm sitting here picking my ear, I wonder if I will get chucked out? I wonder what would happen if I suddenly jumped up swearing and singing and throwing my clothes off? That might put some life back in the old buggers. I don't suppose so, they would probably all murmur lowly down into their drinks, mumble agreement, then get back to their books! Well I am too cold here too, I am going, see you.

Am now back in the cabin, Corries on, now that is good music. I've just looked and my nose is sunburnt, all red like a drunk, at least it will hide the 2 plukes!

I think I'll go for a 'Black Prince cocktail' after dinner (Dinner being tea!). It depends on how everyone else is dressed. If they all stare at me, I'll realise I should have changed into my skirt.

I wore my tartan dress for the Captains Cocktail party last night. Val or whatever you call her, that came to the bingo with me, just stared at me the whole time. I think my black bra straps were showing, oh shock horror. She made a joke to the waiter, later on, about me being in my swimming costume, so I think it must have been a bit revealing. Wait until she does actually see me in my swimming costume, she might fall down dead! Oh that's nasty.

I must have been a bit (to put it extremely mildly!) nastier about people in those days. It must have been early 1993 I think, so I would have been 25. I was young and cynical without my today's lovey, dovey, Pollyanna way with the world. I hate being horrible about people now. But maybe I would be, maybe it was just me being creative and truthful in my diary, after all I didn't expect it to be written into an actual book. I suppose if we all wrote our immediate, innermost thoughts straight down without thought or editing they might not be as nice as the things we actually say. I must say, I did seem to have a rather worrying obsession in the diary with stating that people slept alone.

You know I've spent so many decades living on my own now that I am arriving at the view point that it might not be so bad an idea for a married couple to have separate bedrooms. They could have their own space, a good sleep and still appreciate the excitement of having fun whenever they wanted to 'visit' each other. You'd have to be very careful though as one step in the wrong direction and you could also be living separate lives and then what would be the point in actually being with each other at all. No on second thoughts bring all couples back to the same bed!

I never watch films or go to the cinema (well I do occasionally now when my lovely nephew Jack is here for a visit) so it was a real holiday treat for me to sit in a private booth, in the video lounge and watch a film. I remember watching Ghost and loving it. My film watching was spoiled a bit by a posh passenger walking down the corridor and saying loudly to her partner, "imagine coming all this way just to sit and watch a film".

That comment seemed so rude, intrusive and unknowing of the facts. But now I come to think of it, it is the kind of comment that I would make now about people watching tv, football, using their mobile phones or whatever.

There is a boy, a man I should say, on the bus who sits up the very front of the top deck of the double decker. He opens his lap top up, puts his headphones on and watches films (I presume) the whole of the journey. I can't stand that and think what a waste. He should be busy watching out the window and appreciating our world.

You know the trouble with this book is I can't draw smiley faces to tell you when I am having a wee bit of a joke although I suppose there is always a bit of truth behind it as well so maybe it is good that I can't draw my smiley faces. I'm getting fed up of always typing exclamation marks, so I expect that also means that you are getting fed up seeing them! Oops there was another one.

So the man on the bus is busy watching his screen. Sometimes I think that he looks round thinking that I must be nosing at what he is watching. Actually I am trying very hard not to look at the screen. It really annoys my lovely view out the window to have things moving on a screen in front of me, it draws my eyes to it. It is fine though once I have managed to get lost in my wee world and then I can focus on the view and nothing distracts me.

It was quite funny one time there was another man sitting right at the front of the bus engrossed in his newspaper. He was so busy reading the **news** that he missed the fact that we drove past a quite dramatic real life scene of a car which had skidded off the road and landed down in the trees below. It seemed to me really funny and quite ironic, the things we miss being stuck in our various media items and not actually looking for ourselves at the world. Mind you I also miss an awful lot of things by not keeping up-to-date with all that is going on with society through the media.

I really love quiz nights but seem to be getting worse and worse at them. They don't seem to have good old questions anymore about things like science and nature, food and drink etc. It's all films and music that I am getting more and more out of date with. I used to do my competition magazines which helped me a lot with all the gossip. But when I stopped watching the soaps, I stopped doing my magazines. I used to read them and work through them at the same time as watching the soaps, now I don't have the time to do them I am too busy using the computer or something that I can't do at the same time as reading a magazine.

I stopped watching the soaps when the European football was on. (That was many years ago now.) I got really annoyed when the football was on and ruined the times for my soaps. This resulted in changes in my routines, very annoying. So I decided to give myself a challenge to stop completely watching the soaps for a while. It worked and I found it so nice and refreshing to have about an extra hour and half free every single evening that I stuck at it and have never gone back to watching the soaps since.

So back to my job at Perth College, Kathryn was going off on her big adventure, I'd been on my cruise, I had Granny's money and I was unhappy at work. I decided that I would stop work! What was the point of working 9 to 5 every weekday making a bit of money but never having anytime to enjoy it?

My leaving speech, made by the old Open Learning Department boss, Stewart Duncan, was brilliant. He really caught my character and had us all rolling about in laughter with his mention of my strange customs, such as, if I couldn't be found my desk, I would be on an Aborigine Walk About, when I needed to! Thank you Stewart for that speech, I loved it. I'm not so sure what the (at the time) new Principal thought of it though!

So now I was free. I always look out my kitchen window looking at Drummond Castle, at the hills and beautiful view and sing 'I'm free, free to do what I want any old time.' I sang this a lot at this time and was really happy.

I went a weekend to Wales (a huge step for me) for a 'paranormal' weekend, it was really interesting. I'd never been to Wales before. Grampa Roberts was born and brought up in Wales. It is a place I would still like to visit and go and explore one day.

I took 2 home study courses, 'Dream Analysis' and 'Self Development' which were both interesting and gave me new hobbies for a while. I also did a great course 'Writing for Children'. That is writing children's books as opposed to Children writing books. It was again a really therapeutic course, reading loads of children's books and reliving loads of old childhood thoughts, feelings and memories. I had a whole plan for a book and even wrote the first chapter, having completed all the other initial units, tasks and exercises. But then my tutor started to go on about getting my book published by their company and paying for it. I got suspicious that it might be a con and so like a lot of things I've done, I gave up.

It was my plan to learn to drive and get a car but I never did. I just started my laid back life of routines! Do laid back and routines work together as the one thing? They seem more like opposites to me. Mind you if you disturb my routines then I won't be laid back so I suppose in that way they do.

No waking up with an alarm clock. Alarm clocks should be thrown in a huge pit along with all the mobile phones and blown up. I have to go out everyday for fresh air no matter what the weather otherwise I feel stuffy and like I'm in prison. I'd go up to my Dads to use the Internet. I've got an old dinosaur of a computer at home that my brother gave me but I don't have the Internet. Well I won't pay or couldn't afford the bills. Come to think of it, I don't know if Dad had the Internet yet back then.

It's really strange to try and imagine life without the amazing tool of the Internet. What I love is the way it is a whole world that exists and we can visit but it isn't actually physically there, magic, utter magic.

(I do have the internet now and a lovely laptop computer so the magic world of the web is at my fingertips.)

Anyway I would fill my days with walks, painting, reading, using computers, listening to music etc etc. I love doing art but never get round to it much, another thing that I need a real kick up the bum to get started. I have sold a few paintings over the years.

(You can see some of my artwork at:

http://bspaintings.blogspot.com/

I now have a digital camera and absolutely love going my walks with my camera and getting lost in the magical, wonderful world of nature. You can see some of my photos at:

https://www.facebook.com/BsPhotosWorld?fref=ts
http://bsphotographs.blogspot.co.uk/

It is a brilliant hobby. I would love to spend my life just walking in nature and taking photos. I sometimes wonder if I just like it as it is kind of like a lazy art. I can instantly have a beautiful picture with no effort what so ever. But what does it matter, it captures the magic and I love to get different views and shots that people wouldn't notice as they rush by.

Digital cameras are brilliant because I can take loads and loads of photos to see what happens and not worry at all about using up the film. I'm beginning to wonder if photography is maybe just about the quality of the camera, which is unfair really. Of course there is also the skill of settings, lenses etc. I am not at all into all that. I just want to capture interesting images that I see with my eyes and feel inside me really I suppose.)

I also tended to start new hobbies and in those days, while I still had money. I would buy everything I needed, all the books etc for my new hobby. For example Calligraphy, I got pens, a drawing board, rulers, ink, felt tips and books. I really love the excitement of a new challenge and hobby. But after a few weeks of practising and working non stop, I gradually stop and leave the things ready on my desk for about a year until I finally admit that I better tidy it away for now.

I do the same but much shorter for amazing ideas for books, artwork, creative projects etc. I spend hours that night planning all the incredible details in my head. But by the time I've got it all perfect in my head, I'm not then interested in starting from scratch and doing all the boring actual work.

I wanted to do all the beautiful, brilliant projects in the calligraphy books but my practice writing just didn't seem the same, there was too much of a jump from what I could actually do to the perfection of the show pieces. It's funny I don't feel the same with my piano. I just love to learn and practice and am very happy and pleased with each wee bit of music that I learn. I don't listen to fancy piano music and say oh I can never do that so I'll just give up now. Maybe the difference is that I hear music rather than picture it? I do look at the music notes and think oh I can't read that, with the more difficult ones I don't feel like I'll ever be able to read them. But because I can sit down and play tunes and make lovely noises, practice them and get better with them, I don't give up, I keep trying and learning.

I wish I had had piano lessons when I was a kid. Duncan, my older brother got both piano lessons and horse riding lessons, both of which I was really jealous of. We lived in Dollar then and I was told that I would get the lesson when I was older, we moved to Crieff when I was 10. Our new lives in Crieff were a lot different and I never did get the lessons.

Mind you I maybe wasn't so jealous of the piano lessons at the time. I remember wondering about them because Duncan used to come back in tears from his piano lessons with Mr Foot, I think he was called. I thought at the time that the man must just have been horrible and given Duncan nasty rows. Duncan told me, in recent years, that he actually had been upset as Mr Foot used to be disappointed in him if he hadn't done his best. Duncan is brilliant at music a real natural, he can pick up a wee toy plastic instrument and make a tune out of it. My wee brother Calum is very musical too.

But I did and do manage to do a lot of creative things and love them when I actually get into them. I really love gardening now as well but back then it wasn't one of my choices.

For around a year I lived on my Granny's money with no income. Eventually, as I saw it was dwindling rapidly, I gave in and went to sign on.

I'd been on the dole for a short while before. When I left school, I went to Dundee to study Architecture. I also got a place at Moray House

Edinburgh for Primary Teacher Training. I should have chosen that, Granny would have kept me right. She lived in Edinburgh and I would have made a great primary teacher.

Teaching runs in my family. Granny Roberts, my Mum, my Auntie Ada, Sue (my Step Mum), my brother Duncan, my uncle Jack, my Auntie Willa, my brother Chris, my brother Findlay and his wife Mairi are all or have all been teachers at some time.

But I chose Architecture, it sounded new and exciting, a whole new creative world to explore. I lasted a term. By the end, I was completely miserable and just wanted to come home. Granny wisely suggested that I change over to Art College (I so wish I'd listened) but I didn't, I came home. The classes and lectures started off ok, I would go to some nights out and tried to get on with my flatmates. But then the course work asked for me to make a scale model. I just couldn't. It sounds really simple but for me it wasn't. I thought I was creative and artistic but I didn't seem to be able to come up with new ideas, fitting in to what they asked for. A pretty big problem if I was to do Architecture!

We were asked to create a shelter. Although I did create a model, a very interesting one, it wasn't the neat idea that I had in my head. It was all different bits just stuck together and made into something that would work as a shelter. Maybe it would be easier now with the amazing things that computers can do. Maybe they don't need you to actually physically model make so much now. We had what they called a crit on our models. I missed it as I was skiving off at the time but I was told when I got back that the tutor had picked it up and said "right now to the shrine". This might have been ok if that was what it had been meant to be. I find it really easy now to imagine and create a shelter in my head but I suppose if it came down to the model making it still wouldn't be the same as the amazing things I can picture in my head.

I became miserable, didn't go out socialising so much. I tried to skive off but the landlady's brother would come in to clean the bedrooms and report to the landlady that I wasn't at Uni. I'd become used to being free at home, with no one really bothering about me as long as I did my jobs. But here I was, supposed to be away from home and free, being checked up on and reported. I started skiving off and coming back home for weekends, which just made me more homesick. Not really for my home though as Sue had already cleared out my bedroom, scraped my sticker collection off the bed and redecorated.

Before I left home I think it had become quite confusing for me. Dad would be away from home working a lot. My big brothers had both left home, which I think left me feeling subconsciously abandoned. There was Sue who didn't really bother about me much in those days except to give me my list of jobs and check I'd done them and Findlay who was a brilliant wee chap. I got on great with him and spent a lot of my time babysitting for him. The last year or so there was also Calum still just a wee baby, being 4 years younger than Findlay. In those days Dad was incredibly controlling and although lovely and great fun, could have a terrible temper. I knew that and knew how to deal and cope with that but what really confused me, I think, was that Dad was away so much. I would be left to do exactly what I wanted with no one bothering about me, then Dad would come home and as soon as he was in the house he would start ordering things and laying down his rules again. This state of complete opposites did not fit in with my way of understanding and knowing my world. I think that is probably when I started to withdraw a bit from people and look after and think about myself more, creating my own safe, secure world.

But having left home, I think, perhaps, I was homesick, probably more for my past than for what I'd had at home in recent years. Anyway completely miserable I came home.

I always did get homesick. I would be fine wherever I was, even having great fun, until night time arrived and then it felt terrible. One time a daughter of some family friends we were out at the cinema with, invited me back to her house. I got on great until my Dad arrived with my night things and my womble pillow. (I loved my 'womble pillow'. it was a pillowcase with the wombles on it. The good old original wombles, none of those new ones! I still remember all their names off by heart. Dad still has the womble pillowcase in his house. I don't think he uses it anymore though!) I went to put them in the room I would be sleeping in and that was it I started crying and just wanted my Dad to take me home. It was very embarrassing, I never got invited back. Poor Rachel who asked me to stay must have wondered what on earth happened, so sorry to you Rachel.

I had that same problem everywhere. The only person I could stay with fine was my Granny Roberts.

I had a security blanket 'cuddly' for many years. I remember one time when I was a teenager. I finally decided that it was time to do without cuddly. I put it inside Koala a big red koala cuddly toy I had with a zip on the bottom. It is still there, up in Dad's attic. I wouldn't want to find them now as it would be horrible to throw them out. I have a vague memory of my Mum taking my cuddly away one time and sewing it. I think it must have been getting worn and she folded it over and sewed it up to half its size. There were wee lacy bits folded up like rose buds on it. I loved them. They fitted my fingertips just nice inside them. Cuddly was made of a sort of silky white material with padding stuff underneath. I still love the feel of that kind of silky material.

I have a problem with touching some things. I can't stand things getting caught in the carpet nor people taking woollen gloves off with their teeth. AAAAAAgh, it makes my teeth go funny just to think about it. People talk about making their "teeth curl". Well that's what that does to me. Trust me to have a different thing to what most people can't stand.

I also can't stand things in my clothes like labels rubbing or sticking into me. I often have to take the labels off the collar on t-shirts etc, which is really annoying. They always seem to be sewn in so securely that they can leave wee holes when I try to remove them. I am getting much better at that particular removal skill though, with many years of practice.

So back to me giving up University and arriving back home. Dad, in those days, in no way approved of people doing nothing and definitely **not** of being on the dole. We had a huge argument where I stormed out and drank loads of Martini, a bottle I'd been given when leaving Dundee as a Christmas present.

Tom, Dad's friend was getting a flat but couldn't afford it on his own, so I moved in with him. I was crying and really homesick that first night and never fit in at that first flat. It had a rat hole in the floorboards and I had to wear a scarf round my ears in bed, it was so cold. A year later the flat was to be demolished, so I moved with Tom to the flat that he used to live in, in the middle of town. I felt at home from the very first day in the new flat and have lived here ever since.

In that first flat, I was unemployed for a while. I learned to sleep in late as it saved money on food and passed some of the day away. Babs' sister, Sandra, persuaded me after a month or 2 to get the waitressing job that I described earlier, which I did.

So now, years later (Are you keeping up with the jumping about? I'm back to being unemployed but not that first time, later on after having left my Perth College job.), that Granny's money was rapidly running out, I went back to that horrible Job Centre. I waited a couple of years or so more before I gave in and applied for housing benefit. That was just as a matter of principle but pretty much a waste of money that I could have had, I suppose.

Looking at dates on an old CV, I must have managed to wangle my free unemployed life for quite a few years.

A few years on, I started voluntary training for work. I became a Wildlife Habitat Surveyor. It was brilliant. I got training and studying to do which resulted in an HNC (Higher National Certificate) in Wildlife Habitat Surveying. I loved it. My favourite subject was plant ID. We got to go out walks in woods, by rivers, up hills etc while still getting unemployment benefit. I always thought if the job centre people actually new how happy I was they would have stopped my dole money! I think that they were just happy to have another number to write down on their carrying out training list.

We still had to look for jobs every Friday. I would look through all those brilliant wildlife (of the nature variety) type jobs, in different parts of the world and dream.

It seemed that along with most other interesting type, different jobs, such as archaeology, that the way to get into them was to work as a volunteer. Great if you were, unlike me, brave enough or had enough money to give up your home or carry on paying for that, travel and pay for accommodation and of course have no income while you did work. In fact with the archaeology type ones and also animal surveying, you have to pay ridiculous amounts of money to actually do the voluntary work!

So I enjoyed my year of training, got new dreams to add to my collection and then went back on the dole. Another few years passed by of my life.

One Summer, still keen on the idea of combining Art with wildlife work, I suddenly made a snap decision. Seeing an advert in a wildlife magazine, I applied to do a degree in Wildlife Illustration at Sunderland Art College.

It started very soon after I applied. With no time to think and chicken out, I found myself being driven down by Dad to take an interview and if successful start the course. I got the place and Dad helped me unpack. I cried and cried and didn't want him to go.

They put me in a small room in halls with thin walls where I could hear the people next to me talking all the time. I was completely miserable, got no sleep at all and ended up in a trance like state, just trying to get through each day. I lasted a week before begging on the phone for Dad to come and take me home. The day I was leaving, I got talking to the cleaners.

They showed me a much bigger room off on its' own which would have been nice and quiet. I should have given it more of a go but I didn't. With much relief and a lot of embarrassment, I arrived, so happy to be back, at home and got to sleep in my own wee bed back in the flat which luckily at that time I still rented from Tom and so was still there for me.

Not long after that, I went for a night out with Sandra. I got drunk and Sandra had to take me home. I was in a terrible state and couldn't even get up the stairs to the flat on my own. Sandra got me to go to bed but I started having a panic, not able to breathe and refusing to let Sandra phone my Dad as I would wake him and Sue up. Poor Sandra had a horrible time and ended up phoning for a Doctor to come and see me. He suggested I might have taken drugs.

I knew I hadn't taken drugs and later made sure my own Doctor knew that, as I didn't want it down on my record. I worked out that what I'd had was a really bad panic attack and I decided that I was never ever going to have one again. I wrote down and told my Doctor all about it. He reassured me that I wasn't going mad and suggested that I see a Counsellor.

It cost money and I had very little but she did discount for poorer people and Dad and Sue very kindly volunteered to help me pay. So I had a number of sessions with a very nice lady, a Person Centred Counsellor.

That night out and experience really put me off drinking for a long time, I don't drink alcohol at all now really (I do like a cider at a quiz night!) and never get drunk like I used to. Sometimes I used to walk past a pub at night and get that smell that reminded me of the good old, fun night outs we used to have and wish I was in there but now I don't even feel that. In fact I don't really ever go out at nights, just stay in safe in my wee flat.

As for the counselling, well, I enjoyed it. I don't know if I said what I was meant to say. I got a bit confused at first when I thought it was going well but she said 'I can't help you if you don't talk to me'. I never talked about my Mum dying, I said I felt I was over that, which I believed. Maybe she felt that I that I should have done a lot more work on that.

I remember sitting in the Doctors waiting room, watching the tropical fish. I was really cheery and smiling when my counsellor came to get me while showing her last client out. The other client looked miserable and the counsellor was tidying away a box of tissues. That's when I began to think that I maybe didn't need counselling anymore.

I thought back to my first session when I felt completely 'stuck'. Each session I would write my thoughts down afterwards. Now, thinking back to my thoughts about the previous session, I realised that I had felt how I was moving along a train track again. I remembered and connected how I had felt stuck at first, that's when I decided I could end the counselling.

I remember meeting the counsellor quite a while after that. It was strange as she asked how I was but I realised that I was to ask her how she was as well now. She explained how some clients never talked to her outside the sessions. I realised that giving away your inner most secrets, feelings and darkness must be a thing you want forgotten about and understood why some people might avoid a counsellor later. It must be a lonely profession.

So, not long after my counselling I felt motivated and brave enough to try for a new job. I saw the perfect job at a place nearby. I went for an interview for a weeks work trial and knew straight away, from a feeling, that I'd got the job.

The place supplied blank pottery mugs, plates, ornaments etc. People came in and painted them however they liked and once the pieces were fired, got to take them home. There was also a soft play area for young kids, a café and a bead station where people could choose beads and make jewellery.

I absolutely loved the big containers full of all different textured and brightly coloured beads. My friend has a bead shop. A magic place that just has shelves and shelves of boxes and trays of beads, all different colours, shapes, textures. I could just spend all my time running my fingers through the different beads and sorting the ones in the wrong place into the right place.

Well back to the job. With the mix of art, painting, helping people and working with kids, it was the perfect job for me. Unfortunately it didn't work out like that. The woman (the co-owner) was very confusing. She was thin and I think lived and thrived on being scarily chaotic, fun, angry and busy all at the same time.

I tried my best but got things wrong like I do when I'm muddled and not sure what I'm meant to do. She was having an angry panic in the room where the sink was to fill up the bucket with hot water to wash the floor, so wouldn't let me in. The only other tap I could reach was cold so I just used that with a lot of floor cleaner and got on with the job. When the other staff member came back I told her what I had had to do. She just looked at me like she was completely stunned at my stupidity. She then showed me how I could have got jugs of hot water out the machine for making teas and coffees. Then told me I would have to do the whole job over again.

I was miserable and confused. I just wanted to be back safe at home. I would get home and cry at nights. At dinnertime I would sit at the window and look out at the trees wishing I could be out with them. I got on well with the painting and really enjoyed it. I made a lovely green tile for my Dad with scrabble tiles cascaded on it, spelling out scrabble. A couple came in with their kids, I had great fun playing with the kids and talking to the couple, suggesting ideas about their painting. I said they should do this, suggesting an idea for the painting. The boss came out and in front of the people, said **'we** don't tell the customers what to do'. It was so patronising I couldn't believe it. She was quite a posh lady and when the couple had gone, she said 'that was horrible'! I realised that I had gone into my Scottish 'common' voice which I do sometimes, perhaps a bit over the top but I think the family had really enjoyed themselves.

One day the owners' children were there, they seemed nice, a bit posh, just back from a skiing trip. One was quite young and one quite a bit older. I was tidying up the soft play area when I found a kid had very nicely left a cream egg, with the top bitten off, in the middle of it. I went to the loo to get some paper towels or a cloth and dampen them. I was just squeezing out the water when I looked round and saw the boss' youngest child, sitting there on the toilet staring at me in a very worried way!! The toilet door had been open and the light off. I had not bothered to put it on as the sink was just at the door. I said "oh sorry" and went out, the older kid was outside the door also just staring at me!! I explained what I had gone for and that I hadn't known she was in there but I dread to think what the boss must have thought if she heard that story from them!!

At the end of the week the boss said she was looking for a team member and I hadn't fitted in. I actually thought that I had started to get used to them and do a bit better but never mind I was out of there and that was that.

In later years, meeting an acquaintance who had also worked there and done really brilliant before getting promotion and moving on to work with that particular boss, then hearing about how that ruined it all, really helped me to understand that the problem hadn't been with me. That made me feel so much better from a personal view point.

So it was back to the good old Job Centre. After a while (quite a while), I had been unemployed for so long that I was allowed to go on 'Back to Work Training'. I got a brilliant year's placement with the Scottish Wildlife Trust. I loved it. But I've told you about that already. It is hard enough to write a book with a computer when you can do Search and Find if you think you have written something already. Imagine how hard it must have been when it was just typing or even writing! What magic things computers are. I love computers, hours fly by when I am using them. I always think when you find things that make time disappear that they are the things you should do as a career.

I could only do that Wildlife Habitat Surveying for a year, so it was back to the Job Centre. After another long time, I was getting threatened with horrible jobs again. It was the day, when I was asked if I wanted to apply to work in a burger van that I realised I was going to have to find some training to do again. Somehow I managed to arrange to go on a course at College for Complementary Therapies full time and use it as training for work.

I got a very neat and un-me white dress uniform to wear and got started at the College. It was a great and very interesting experience. We got to learn and study loads of things such as massage, aromatherapy, reflexology, counselling and psychology. We even got to study some chemistry. I had always thought I hated chemistry. Mr Cuthbert, our school Science teacher that I told you about, once gave us a chemistry lesson. It was probably designed to get us really interested in Chemistry but it just frightened me and put me right off. He went into his wee office and into the glass cupboard while we stood and watched, safely, through the other side of the glass. He put some chemicals together and made a spectacular explosion.

In a lesson way it maybe didn't work as I have no idea what he did or what chemicals he used. All it taught me was that chemistry was really dangerous and that I didn't want to do it. But when we got Chemistry at College I was really surprised that I really enjoyed and found it very interesting. I was fascinated that everything was made up of things and could be broken down and put together in different ways and react in different ways. A brilliant subject, I wish I had taken it at school!

So I learned a lot and really enjoyed my Complementary Therapies year. It was great fun and very therapeutic. The goal had been to start doing my own business after that using the skills I had gained. But I didn't. It just gives me that empty feeling starting something without knowing exactly how and what to do step by step. Perhaps I could have got a job at some salons but they all seemed to be beauty therapy orientated just not my style. Later many more therapy type places were opening but I just didn't have the confidence or motivation for doing the job. Another one that was safe to dream but never actually do.

Now I love my wee flat but we have had some very noisy and upsetting neighbours as in the horrible fights that they have had. The neighbours we have at the moment are ok. They are a bit rough and occasionally have loud arguments or fights but nothing like what we were getting. One family that lived there used to have frequent fights with horrible, loud, scary shouts, screams, bangs and noises that sounded like things and people getting thrown about.

The fights and arguments scare and really upset me. They disturb my nice peaceful world. I feel bad at not phoning the police sometimes but it is too scary to get involved and also I don't want to be interfering. At least I am lucky that it is nothing to do with me and I am safe and cosy behind my big, solid, good old-fashioned front door.

I know nowadays there are loads of adverts and campaigns that it is up to us to help if we suspect anyone is being abused at all. This is a great idea but I don't know if the campaigners realise just how scary it would be to get involved even anonymously? I am glad that those campaigns weren't around then. Also although the members of that family must have had a really horrible time, to put it extremely mildly, they were also a really close family and looked after each other. But then I suppose you would have to if you had to live with that and you would have to avoid outsiders getting too close. But that is maybe another reason that it would actually be a good idea to get outside professional help involved? Still it was not something that I would have felt comfortable enough doing. It's always easier just to hide and hope that someone else will make the effort. The easy way isn't the best way to live life but at least in the short term, it is the easiest way! I wonder if that way leaves me feeling much more depressed and unfulfilled than making an effort and making changes would? Probably. Life is an interesting and funny or rather strange balance.

The 2 sisters from that family used to sometimes be out in the garden and I got to know them just to say hello to. I would try to act normally if it was a day after a bad fight night.

Sometimes I would do painting out in the garden, so I could sit out in the fresh air and enjoy the lovely sun. They would come up to see what I was doing. One of the girls told me about how she would go up to the

Community Learning Centre and help out there doing voluntary work. Hearing that, made me stop in my tracks and think that if she had all her troubles and could do that then I, a lazy unemployed waster, could and should do something too. I had often looked at the ads for voluntary work but never been brave enough to do anything about it. I don't like the feeling that I will be trapped in something if I start. I suppose it is the being out of control that I subconsciously can't cope with. But that girl went through hell and still was brave enough to do voluntary work. So I went to find out about it.

I started doing a teaching adults how to read course, which I really enjoyed. I gave it up though, I can't remember why. It probably got too scary and real for me as they were talking about getting someone to work with and just getting on with it on our own.

A year later I decided to be brave and have another go. The course I had been on had moved to Perth, so being unemployed, I couldn't afford the travelling for that and wasn't brave enough anyway. But I got an interview with a lady about what I might be interested in doing. I gave a list of things and explained about my interests in children, one to one work, dyslexia, education etc. I got a few leaflets and lists of things I might like and some looked good but I didn't have the nerve or motivation to go to the places and start.

Quite a while after this, the volunteer co-ordinator contacted me with an idea. She told me about and I agreed to go with her to see a wee boy and his family who needed some help. The minute I went into Alexander's house and met his large chaotic family, I felt at home and knew I wanted to do this. He had trouble with co-ordination and speech and I was to get to know him, and then work with him on his exercises.

I really enjoyed my work with Alexander. His family were lovely as well. His Mum invited me along with them to the physical therapy class near Edinburgh to see how it worked. It was really interesting and I wanted to do that kind of work as my career.

I ended up doing a lot of art type work with Alexander. He loved to paint and make a mess and would say his words, read and things as he was doing his 'work' with me. At first he had to be dragged into the room with me and often got a row from his parents but soon he was cheery and really looking forward to our time together. He loved to paint with black paint and I would let him just paint all over the page if he wanted. It was a shame because his Mum ended up taking the black paint away to get him to use other colours. I didn't feel it was my place to say that it was the idea for Alexander to paint and use whatever colour he wanted over and over to get things out of his system.

Because I was unemployed and doing voluntary work, I couldn't be paid but they used to ask me to baby-sit for all the kids and would give me a bit of money for that which came in really handy. When you are living on unemployment benefit, even just an extra £10 is an amazing amount of money and really helpful.

(Nowadays I, like most people, don't think much of people who just stay unemployed and don't do anything but I hope I am getting you to see and think about the thoughts and feelings that could be behind some of these people (even if just a few) and how not all of them are just lazy. They are all individuals and all have their own ways and reasons for being and doing what they do or don't do.

I also can't understand at all the discussions that go on now about capping benefits when they talk about thousands of pounds. How can people be on benefits and get so much money? I lived on very little money with job seekers allowance and only got a portion of my rent paid with housing benefit. Having so little money was a choice that not working brought. I realise that our thoughts are why should people get money when they don't work for it but it was so little and that is what I don't understand when people go on about the capping of benefits. As a single unemployed person it was almost impossible to buy things and it certainly wouldn't have worked with the price of food, heating, travel etc today.)

Alexander's Mum told me about a club being opened up at Muthill (a nearby village) for kids on the autistic spectrum. I started volunteering there and really loved it. I did it for a few years. We did an after school club and then a holiday club in the school holidays. It was a great experience working with and getting to know the kids, their different characters and ways of doing things.

Our best day out was a day white water rafting!! It was very chaotic. I don't think the instructor had realised just quite what a raft of autistic spectrum kids involved!! But it was a brilliant experience with just a few tears and dangerous moments along the way.

These volunteer jobs were excellent for me getting actual job interviews and adding work experience to my CV. I also did some work at the After School Club in Crieff. It was an actual job but because I was unemployed, the money I earned was taken off my dole money, so I was working for no pay. Again this experience really helped to get me a job.

Finally I got a job at Comrie After School Club. Because it wasn't many hours, it wasn't much pay but still a lot more than the dole. I really enjoyed the work. It suited me well getting back to work without doing 9 to 5. It is really therapeutic working with kids, having fun and playing!! I reckon everyone should have to do it. Compulsory punishment for crabby adults, who have lost their magic and hate kids!!

The boss was a lovely lady and gave me a lift in her car to work and back, which made things much easier time ways and also as I had very little money for the bus. She was great and loved craft and art things, so it was great fun working with her. But I found her quite confusing and scary at times. She was very calm and laid back but at times she would go in moods and that was scary and confusing for me.

Having grown up in a house of males, we all just shouted at each other when we were angry. But my new boss wouldn't let me shout. She would tell me lots of things at once and I'd get all confused and start doing one thing to make her happy when she would change it and tell me to do something else or do it another way. I would get angry and then start to shout. I very, very occasionally get angry but when I do, I explode and can feel it thumping in my head. But she wouldn't let me shout, she would say, "just don't". Then if I tried to talk calmly about it she would refuse to carry on the conversation. This was really strange, confusing and frustrating for me. However, it was also a really good lesson and development for me, as I had no choice but to calm down and get on with something else. A new and different way of dealing with anger, not my way, but an interesting new view point.

I loved my job and the kids but was still looking for and applying for a full time, better job. The club was due to shut down anyway. So I carried on getting interviews but not getting any actual jobs. Then I finally managed to get myself a job as a Learning Support Assistant at Perth Grammar.

But before I tell you about Perth Grammar, I don't think I ever actually told you about the 2 weeks I HAD to go to the Job Club in Perth. That compulsory 2 weeks in the July I was telling you about. It was 3 summers ago now (or was when I wrote this paragraph, now many more) and the last time we seem to have had any summer at all. We had the strangest heat wave that I can remember. Well except for the hot long summers as a kid, where the pavements were too hot to stand on with bare feet, but then summers are always longer and hotter in memories aren't they?

Anyway it was the hottest weather I can remember here in Scotland. It was so hot we got sent home early a couple of days as it was illegal to keep us in the building. It was well over the actual official level of comfort. The trouble was there is a gap in the buses in the afternoon so I was set free from the job club but couldn't get home aaaaagh!!

We had to go in everyday all day for 2 whole weeks and do things like watch videos on how to do job interviews and be told how to make CVs. It was all stuff I had done a million times before and all dragged out to make it fit the days. There were some really interesting characters there. There were some 'bad people' a couple of them were off certain days or didn't come back as they were due in court. Not long after that, one of the people that I had been talking to when using the job club, was in the news having been arrested for stalking a woman and was banned from being alone with females. This was actually a very scary thought and feeling. But they were all real characters and they got more interesting the more I got to know them over the days. Two of them would sit with a game of chess out in front of them on the table and they all had interesting life stories. I came to the conclusion that there are a lot of intelligent (not necessarily educated and in some cases very educated), interesting people who just can't or find it very difficult to cope with some parts of society and fitting in with the drudgery, rules and restrictions of ordinary day in day out jobs. Including myself!!

It was very frustrating being made to go there every day and be re-taught all these basic getting a job, common sense skills. However to make it even worse, I had actually heard that I had got myself the job at Comrie After School Club. I went round to the job Centre and pleaded with them not to make me suffer sitting in that prison all those days in that heat wave. But they wouldn't let me away with it. Their argument was that my job didn't start until the new school term and it was still just July, so I might not start it. I grumpily gave in and went back to the 'prison'!! It was quite fun in some ways. I enjoyed getting to know the characters, watching what the staff had to do and how they dealt with people and some of the team building exercises. Also even for a sun loving, fresh air, fiend like me, it would have really been too hot that fortnight to actually have been outside for long anyway. So, with no choice, I stuck with it.

So further on, here I was with a job at Perth Grammar school. It was terrifying to think of going to work in a huge high school, much larger than the one I had gone to myself and packed full with teenagers. I get on brilliantly with wee kids but by the time they get to primary 7 and above, they start to look at me with despair and, I think, find me not only embarrassing but also a bit bewildering!!

When I started the job, I found out that it wasn't actually a learning support assistant, as the job had been advertised, but a behavioural support assistant. So I worked with the kids that were really bad and had been put out of classes. I loved it. A lot of it was one to one work which really suited me. I even got to start some Art Therapy type work with some of them. We sometimes got to play games like Monopoly, which some staff didn't approve of but I thought was brilliant. It taught the pupils skills like having to get on with people using play as a tool, counting such as using the dice and the money and learning to cope with not always winning or getting their own way. It made me think that play therapy would also be a brilliant career as well as art therapy.

I liked it best when I got to work with a kid on my own and got to do something peaceful or fun like a game or art, so that they would eventually start talking and relax more. It was usually when there were other people about, either very strict staff or other kids to show off to, that there was trouble.

The job went very well, I loved it and the holidays were brilliant as well. But sadly I got told that the job was ending due to lack of funding. It was a big shock for me. I loved the job. One day I was phoned and asked to go down to see my boss. I went down and she was there with a higher up person. They asked me to sit down and told me that as I knew it had always been a temporary job and they were afraid that they could no longer afford the post. I was very shocked. I said that it wouldn't have been so bad if I hadn't loved the job so much. I then said that I was fine and left the room. I had to go to the loos then as I was crying. Getting myself together I then went back to the room that I had been working in and got back on with my work, letting my pupil do some drawing instead of the work he was supposed to be doing. I didn't tell anyone there what had happened I didn't feel close enough to them in case it would make me cry. But by the next day my boss had told them. So I worked my notice and then left.

I went back later in the year for a couple of days to do some Learning Support supply work, which was much more classroom based. I really enjoyed that as well, it was a great laugh. Once more unemployed, it was to be for no money again. A full time job doing came up, which I applied for but I never heard anything about it. I don't know what happened, the Council always got back to you even if it was a thank you but no thank you. Maybe my application got lost in space somewhere in the processing system. It mustn't have been meant. I also applied for a school library assistant job there. The interview went brilliantly I didn't get the job. The person who used to have the job returned and she got it back. The

Deputy Headmaster (I don't suppose it's politically correct to call him that now but I'll be a sinner!) very nicely phoned me up personally to tell me that I hadn't got it. He said I had done a brilliant interview and if it had been possible he would have given me the job. Experiences and feedback like that really cheer me up, reassure and motivate me a lot.

I applied for lots of school type jobs and got loads of interviews, which I was told I did very well in, but I didn't get any of the jobs. Eventually I heard about my old Desk Top Publishing job coming back up at Perth College. So after a wee bit of advice and persuasion from my friends Helen and Dolores who work there and my nephew Jack who was on holiday with me at the time, I went for it.

About 3 or so years before I had gone for the same job which I didn't get, I don't know if that had anything to do with the fact that the old boss was still there. I heard later that I had done very well at the interview and was nearly picked. So here I was applying for it again and this time, old boss safely having left, I got it.

So now I am back doing my old DTP job at Perth College. Its ok, I love the work, can do it fine and the time flies past. The money is brilliant, they all moan about their pay but after living on the dole over all those years I can't believe how much money I get. The people I am working with are lovely as well but I get very fed up at times because they are so quiet. I say things and they just ignore me, they are just busy working but it makes me feel unvalued and unloved. I tell myself that everyone has their own life and world to get on with and I should just get on with mine but it gets me fed up.

I have got into my nice routines. I go for a wee walk for fresh air each break and lunchtime, get my cups of water to keep me going and go to the canteen for my lunch. When I got back from my first holiday they had moved my desk. I am now facing the window and can open it for fresh air whenever I want, which I love. The only trouble is my computer screen can be seen by the whole room and people who walk in the door, which is not good for checking my emails or having a wee shot of the internet!

(We have now moved round the room again and have some nice new people in here to work with although it can still be deathly quiet at times. They speak and listen to me more which is great and we all have a good laugh at times. They are fine with my strangeness and silliness and I make them laugh at times which is great.)

For the second half of each morning and afternoon, I listen to a great internet radio. I can put in a selection of music that I like and it will play and store a library of my likes. It is a great thing and the music really passes the hours of work away. I sometimes get sore itchy ears and know that the ear plugs are no good for them but I have finally found a type that seems to be comfy enough but also hard enough coated that I don't get sweaty ears and can use them fine mostly. I am very careful to keep the volume quite low so that I can still hear a bit what's going on and not annoy anyone with the noise. Headphone escaping noise is almost as annoying as whispering. I hate whispering, I either want to hear something or not, nothing in between.

I managed to get my desk placed in an even better place now. It is side on to the window. I can get air at times when people can cope with it and also get to see out the window which I love. I have angled the blinds just right so they don't cause a draft or let sun shine on to anyone else and I can still peek out them to see the world. I really hate when occasionally someone shuts the blinds at night because I have them just at the perfect angle.

It is a good room and a good job. I have really settled in now and have managed to be in this job for over 2 years which is really good going for me. Of course I still have my dreams and really just want loads of money so I can escape to a wee house near the sea and woods where I can paint, walk, take photos, explore, love the world and maybe even write all in peace and wonder.

(We have moved rooms since that I have been back here 7 years now (at time of writing the longest I have ever been in any job) there have been one or 2 disasters with job cuts and horrible, upsetting and depressing times. I lost my full time job at the same time as facing the major surgery that I mentioned earlier the 2 things weren't connected at all but I had to deal with them together. My job went down to 2 days with again very little money to live on. Loving and being so settled in this job there was no way I was ever going back or anywhere near that horrible job centre again. So I stuck with it here and now am doing 3 days a week which really suits me well. I would love my full time job back of course but it is perfect in that I get days off to follow my interests and hobbies and then only have to work 3 days a week and get a good enough wage for that although I am back to having to be very careful with my money and not being able to save.)

So that's my career path a huge big circle starting back nearly at the beginning again. I'm funny with the people at work. I think that I am just a bit strange. I go about on my own and really enjoy just doing my own things and thinking away about life. But I also can get very lonely and fed up about not really having friends and people in my life. I do have a lot of friends but they all have their own lives and expect me to come to them which I should make the effort to do but of course I don't. I just get home and get on with my own things.

I listen to a lot of the people sometimes when it's busy in the staff room talking about things and find it quite funny. They are either complaining about people or things like lazy people on benefits!! Or they go on about their houses and other people's houses what's right and what's wrong. I would never want them to see my very 'characterful' flat! With Tom's stripy orange and white sitting room wall! Apparently walls are meant to be cream no question about it. (It is funny rereading this, I have now, after over 20 years of renting the flat from Tom, finally managed to buy it myself. I am very slowly bit by bit doing it up. Probably now my topic of conversation, to those close to me, is quite often about decorating. The sitting room doesn't have stripy orange and white walls anymore but it does have interesting colours and I am still not sure that 'they' would like the sound of it.)

Another future comment, I just want to let you know that I have actually got quite used to going to the staffroom now as part of my daily routine after my walk outside. I never have more than about 5 to 10 minutes there, it is far too stuffy a place anyway hot and with no outside looking windows. It can be a bit serious and boring occasionally depending on the group of people that are in there but mostly I really love my wee visits. It is probably me who can be too loud for some people now. We often do a crossword which I really enjoy, the quick clues **not** the impossible cryptic ones!! At other times we just have a good chat which I also enjoy. I do fine at taking part and joke away having fun and making serious comments and views as well. They often say hello to me when I come in and goodbye when I leave which is really nice.

So I do want to have fun and talk to people I enjoy hearing about people and their lives but am mostly not in the slightest bit interested in the same things as them, or so it seems. So am I different? Most definitely.

As I was saying, I have a job again now and am back in the real world. It is ok, fine and good to have money. But I am just no good at fitting in. I don't know when to say things. I feel like I am intruding or being nosy. I just get interested in something that sounds fun or interesting when listening to other people talking and I make a comment then they will either stop the conversation, roll their eyes or just make a very short comment in answer as if I'm interrupting and stop the conversation or carry on with it without me. These things get me really confused and upset enough to bring me to tears at times. (The new room atmosphere is much better than this and I don't have this problem nearly as much. Once people get used to me they actually seem to enjoy having me as part of the conversation. Well there are still some people at times in certain situations who don't but that is life and all people are different.)

I talked about how much I loved my job at the Grammar school but I didn't fit in or make friends with the people in the office or staff base there either. As usual I got on great with the staff but found them far too quiet and although they did have a good laugh at times, far too serious and sensible.

It sounds like I can't cope with people and am useless socially. I do however actually get on really well with people, have lots of friends and am fun and a great laugh. My friend Helen was just recently telling somebody how I will talk to anyone. She hears someone talking away on the bus and then realises it's me and whatever person I'm sitting next to on the bus, deep in conversation.

I find that I can become friends with or at least get to know anybody really, it just takes time. I worked for 2 and half years at the factory

Lyndalware and it wasn't until the very end that I had finally managed to be accepted by everyone. I quite enjoy the challenge of getting to know and understand people, taking time to get to know them, the way they are and how they act. I think that I have lost that a bit over the years. I tend to hide away and avoid people rather than taking the chance to try that challenge. I still don't like what I call false people, these to me are people, who are really nice but then suddenly will go horrible. I realise that it is to do with them and their moods that they let affect other people but that is not something I like. It confuses me and makes me sad, upset and then I avoid them instead of just realising that it is not personal.

I have my wee routines now and go for a nice walk in the fresh air, through the trees, at break times, which I really love. I can work and am working and I definitely never want to go back to that job centre but I'm just not interested in using my life up working. People always say, 'well neither do any of us want to work'. I think that is true in a lot of cases but I'm not sure if it would suit a lot of people being unemployed.

I was just enjoying my Sunday walk today, loving the world and looking at it's beauty and magic with some rare (at the moment) bit of sunshine beaming down through the leaves of majestic trees. That is the world I want to be in, taking photos, looking at and feeling the magic of nature. I don't want that as my 'job' I just want that as my life.

But I know I'm lazy or at least I don't seem to have the motivation to get on with my painting or writing this book. If I get on then maybe I could make all this a life for myself and be happy but I don't, so do I want it? What do I want? What do you want? It is a hard question when you really get into it and try to make it real.

Part 3

My "Funny" Head

My nephew, as I mentioned earlier, is on the Autistic Spectrum and has Asperger Syndrome, or as clearly as they can define it, that is what he has. He is a great lad (man now) I get on brilliantly with him. It seems that a lot of us Haddows have strange and different problems that fit in with Jack's but poor old Jack has had a much worse time of it.

He, at the age of 14, had a terrible year, refusing to go to school and taking out his anger at not being able to live with his Dad, on his Mum. He was getting violent and controlling towards her, she needed help and told us all but nothing changed until finally it all came to a horrible head and Jack was actually taken away from home and put in a 'home for bad boys'. This was a terrible experience for a young confused, angry, scared, upset autistic teenager. Luckily it seems to have resulted in Jack getting a terrible and horrible fright, being allowed to return home and promising to get back into school. He is doing great at the moment and has even got himself a wee part time job for a few hours a week. I am very proud of him and hope that it continues to go great for him. (This was written a number of years ago. He has had many troubles and traumas over the years going round and round in circles with his worries, anger, memories and attitudes but overall he has done great, does his best and turned into a good, caring man who knows right from wrong and knows how to behave and work hard.)

So because of Jack and also because I always had an interest in such things as the autistic spectrum, dyslexia etc I started reading lots of books on the matter. I especially love books about lives of people dealing with having these kinds of 'differences'.

Reading a book called 'Loving Mr Spock' by Barbara Jacobs was very thought provoking. There are some interesting questionnaires in that book. I know these 'quizzes' are, like the ones found in ladies magazines, very limited in what they can show you. In these multiple choice type quizzes, I always seem to want one extra choice that is in between 2 of the options given or I want to choose 2 or I want to choose bits of one choice but not all of it. This could be an interesting point in the start of my descriptions of myself in that I realise that other people don't take the tests too seriously and it doesn't really matter if the questions don't fit but I find it very troubling if I choose one answer that doesn't quite fit what I feel.

The book 'An Exact Mind' by Peter Myers, discusses how Peter had trouble answering a simple question as it had too many possible answers and was too general. It mentions that when answering such questions the problem may be both in the lack of empathy in not 'getting' what is being looked for and also not being able to narrow down an area if there are no specific rules.

Anyway in the 'Loving Mr Spock' book I read, it had a questionnaire entitled 'sixty indications of Asperger's Syndrome'. I tried the test myself and found the results very interesting. So then I took the test up to try it out with my Dad and Step Mum Sue. I told them I wanted to try a quiz just as a matter of interest and didn't tell them what book it was from, what it was about, nor the area that it was from. They said afterwards that they had just assumed it was something from one of my psychology type books.

So Dad, Sue and I sat down going through the questions and very carefully discussed and chose the answer that best fitted each of us, then I tallied up the scores at the end. It was very interesting, Sue scored 19, Dad scored 65 and I scored 71. I then told them what it had been about and read out how a high score is over 60 points and that "a high score is merely an indication of the possibility of a diagnosis of Asperger's Syndrome". We found this very interesting especially how Sue scored so remarkably different from us which definitely fits in with our characters.

Another part of that book that stood out for me was the description of a thing (I'd never heard of before) called CAPD (Central Auditory Processing Disorder) which apparently causes problems with understanding and responding to the spoken word.

I absolutely hate listening to talking on the radio. It is just a noise to me. I suppose it is a bit like when a parent tells their kid to turn their music down as it is a 'terrible noise'. But for me it is talking that does it. I can listen to it if I really concentrate but it takes an awful lot of effort. Also when someone is talking to me, I find it much easier if I look away and kind of focus but not actually see a fixed point so then I can concentrate on what they are saying easier. This often results in the person thinking that I am not listening to them when actually I couldn't be listening harder.

I have come to believe over the years that us Haddows (Sue is a Haddow and has been since 1977!! But she doesn't fit into these categories so I don't count her in this) have created, without knowing it, an actual Haddow language. It jumps and cuts off people when they are speaking not to be nasty but (I think) because we have already worked out what is going to be said and don't want to have to make the huge effort to listening to the rest of it. Also we don't get the right words so might say the 'thingy' or 'twirly twisty thing' or whatever and know what the other person is talking about. Sue doesn't seem to be able to do this and we can never quite work out if she really can't or if she just finds it annoying! We definitely don't do it to be annoying.

Dad and I have a number of times, tried the experiment of having a conversation where we are not allowed to interrupt and have to wait until the other person has finished what they are saying. This ends up feeling totally strange and stilted also I find I have about five things I wanted to say that I thought of as he was talking, so have to try to remember them for the end by putting fingers up to count them. It is incredibly difficult to remember the things by the time the other person has stopped talking.

The description of CAPD mentions how there can be trouble with telephone conversations. As my brothers Duncan and Christopher (Jacks' Dad) often point out, Haddow's are not very good with telephones. I am getting better at making calls. Although I absolutely hate if someone says 'I will call you' but that is because I hate waiting for the phone to ring, perhaps because it is out of my control? But anyway the real big trouble I have with phones is taking messages. I just hate it. I always get it wrong. People always say oh you'll get better with practice but after many years of phones at various jobs I never have. I find it easy if they tell me a message and it's like a wee story so I can think about it and remember it and write it down after. But if there is a name, address, title, place name etc to take note of I get lost.

The book 'An Exact Mind' mentions how Peter Myers avoids using telephones, one of the reasons given is that the 'social interaction element is too difficult for him to do fluently'. I find the 'fluently' word interesting for my situation the next paragraph discusses this.

The other part of the description about CAPD mentions trouble with face to face conversations especially stressful situations. If someone is hurrying me my words just don't come out, my head goes a complete blank and I have no idea what I was to say. The same happens if someone asks me to do something or get something quickly, something that I am not used to, I completely panic and just can't do anything. Sometimes in shops I can't get my words out right, especially if I have been planning what I was going to say and yet my speech is fine, very good in fact, in normal situations.

I also have big trouble for instance at work or at a family gathering when there are a number of people having a discussion. First of all it is almost impossible for me to get myself listened to. I can say things over and over until I give up at being ignored. Then if people do start to listen or I have actually managed to make a good point I then go and spoil it by wanting to say more but not being able to get the words out or muddling up what I am saying. It is like they all rush together in my head and can't come out at once. So then I say something like 'oh shut up Blanche' and the conversation carries on without me.

The reason I started back on my book tonight is that I am completely and utterly fed up at the moment of being taken for granted and not listened to. That is both at work and at home with my family. I do fine when it is one to one. Today at training I was sitting there becoming more and more frustrated and furious. The computer wasn't working right but I couldn't get the tutor to listen to me to sort it out. Then they were carrying on trying to solve problems and questions and I wasn't getting to think about them as I couldn't try them out until the computer was sorted.

We also had to listen to a computerised tutorial on the computer with headphones. The man's voice was really slow and there was no way I could concentrate on him. I was nearly in tears for something not at all important and no one has any idea I was feeling like that. Then later on back in the office they were all discussing something and I told them about 5 times that we had an email about that earlier. None of them listened to me or acknowledged me at all, which made me feel even worse. Now I know that sometimes I say the wrong things or say things that other people seem to think have no connection whatsoever (because of my picture head?). Perhaps people find it easier to ignore me than try to 'get me' but it really hurts. I feel useless, unneeded and unwanted. I then just want to hide away and not bother about people at all.

(It is strange reading back over this I sound like a real moany groany. I would never usually say all these things and thoughts to people. Writing this book is obviously very therapeutic and cathartic (I knew that word but had to get it right with the help of google) you should give your own book a go.)

Most of the time I cope with this by being a joker and making people laugh. This works well unless people are busy or trying to concentrate when, of course, it just annoys them or they switch off listening to me, starting me back at square one. I've just thought about that saying "square one", I wonder if it comes from sliding back down the snakes in Snakes and Ladders?

There are lots of things I get muddled, which I started taking a note of when I got interested in dyslexia and wondered if I might have that. I sound like a right hypochondriac but it's not that I want something 'wrong' with me I am just really interested in why I seem to be different, even in the fact that the things I have 'wrong' don't seem to fit in to any neat categories.

Wondering about all this at College, I got a test done to see if I had dyslexia. There must have been something interesting in the initial test results as I got a further test with an Educational Psychologist. But the result was that I **didn't** have dyslexia. In fact I found his letter reviewing the results so embarrassing that I hid it away in my drawer for years and didn't show anyone. But now that I re-read it I find it another interesting description of just how I am different.

Here is what he wrote:

21/10/2000

Blanche Haddow, Student at Perth College

I was asked to assess Blanche because her exam results do not appear to reflect her true potential. I gave her reading and spelling tests and dictation, looked at examples of her work and at associated areas of difficulty, discussed her difficulties with her and had access to the Bangor

Dyslexia Test given by Mrs Miller.

Blanche told me that she was regarded as a good student in school. She was good at maths, which she enjoyed. But she did not get the expected results in her exams. Later she did an HNC and an HND but again did not do as well in the exams as she expected. Her siblings have apparently all done well at University.

I gave Blanche a reading test consisting of individual words and another test consisting of continuous text. She had no problems with the reading except that she did not follow all of the text. She told me that she usually follows what she reads. Sometimes she prefers to read things aloud in order to understand them; "it seems to make more sense that way", she said. She loves to get absorbed in reading. From all the evidence Blanche has no problems in reading.

Blanche made few spelling errors in the test. She managed words such as miscellaneous, exhibition, moustache. In the dictation she correctly dealt with magnificently, enthusiasm, unconquered. The few errors she made were all logical and intelligible eg acomplished/accomplished, necessety/necessity, insecent/incessant. In the work Blanche submitted she expressed herself well and there were few errors.

Blanche was quite quick in her approach to the test though there were some hesitations over individual words. She occasionally said that "it doesn't look right" and she had then to make a guess. She found the dictation challenging, having to think about all the words. She finds note taking "annoying" because she has to concentrate on the writing rather than on what is being said.

Blanche showed me a list of miss spelt words which she had written in her school jotter when she was 6 or 7. They showed some letter confusion and many attempts were very phonic but they were not untypical of children of that age.

We looked at associated areas of difficulty. Blanche does not remember confusing b/d or left/right. She can follow directions and give them if she is sure she knows the place. She cannot remember any problems with learning to tell the time or tying laces or ties. (Actually I've later written on the paper that I remembered being late with both laces and time. I remember being at my friend (Linda)'s house and asking what the time was. Her Mum was surprised I couldn't tell the time and pointed out that Linda's' wee brother Peter could already tell the time. I also remember having to get an older girl in the playground to tie my shoe laces for me.)

She describes herself as "rubbish at sport" but does not feel she has any co-ordination problems. She claims to be "very organised in a messy way"; though not particularly tidy she knows where everything is and she doesn't really have any problems with organisation.

We briefly looked at modes of learning. Blanche told me that she loves art and she pictures everything. She likes to have time to look at things and to pick out details. But she also has a good auditory memory; she can sometimes remember conversations word for word. However, she finds it hard to concentrate purely on listening. In fact she "hates listening to just talking on the radio". She has to switch it off. She says she learns best by "trying to work things out, thinking what it means". She needs to understand things before she can remember them.

Blanche says she definitely looks at things in a different way to other people. She reads questions, thinks she understands them but then finds everyone else has taken a different interpretation. She finds this in listening as well as reading. It is interesting that she says she does not enjoy poetry or short stories; she likes longer books that she can become absorbed in. She enjoys books but is "not interested in seeing what's behind them". Other people don't always understand her and she has given up trying to explain because she feels her ideas are complex and she can't always get them across to others. (I have underlined and questioned the word 'complex' here and written myself that 'I get muddled trying to say what I want to say', so that is why I give up.)

The results of the Bangor Dyslexia Test are not indicative of dyslexia and the fact that she does not have real difficulties with reading, spelling, maths or in associated areas would suggest that Blanche is not dyslexic. However it seems that her mind works in a different way to others and this makes her approach to reading and study different at times, of course, challenging and perhaps problematic.

Recommendations: *Blanche feels she does not need any extra help in connection with this course. However she would like to know more about herself and about her thoughts and how she expresses them. It is difficult to know how she can achieve this except through discussion with others and through reading relevant materials. I wish her well in her quest.*

So there you go!!! I DON'T have dyslexia, thank goodness! I did once however, do a test with a family friend whom has been an English Teacher and worked with dyslexic students. She came up with the result that I do 'have a kind of listening dyslexia that I have subconsciously found ways of dealing with over the years, except for telephones which I have learned to deal with by avoiding'.

Another thing I felt was a bit misleading, for me, with the test was that it was taken in a quiet room, with only the man asking me questions where I was really concentrating and interested in what I was doing. It is completely different for me if there are a load of people or if someone is hurrying me and asking me to read, listen to or say something quickly then the wall goes down and I have a complete and utter blank.

A very extreme example of that was when I was in a bad car crash. A police officer took me aside to ask for my report and asked me my address. At the time I sometimes still put my Dads address on some of my things like bank things, even though I didn't live at home. My head must have thought about this as I just couldn't work out what address to say and then panicking couldn't remember my address (at all) not a bit of either of them. It must have seemed very strange to the police officer when I just stood there not being able to tell them my address. Luckily a local police officer, who lives near my Dad, very nicely came over and said, "it's ok I know this person and I know her address". So thank you to him, he really saved my confused head.

If anyone shows me greetings cards with a lot of writing on them on the outside that are meant to be funny, I dread it, especially when there are a number of people there. I used to just not be able to make any sense of the cards at all even though I can read perfectly well. But I have found a trick that really helps a lot with that problem is that I read the card out loud and I seem to be able to understand it better. That story is what the psychologist must have picked up on when he made one of his comments in the report, but it didn't quite fit the right context the way he put it.

I can give directions but I usually avoid it if I can. I remember one time sending a lorry driver the opposite direction than the one he should have gone. He wanted either Auchterarder or Aberfeldy and I sent him to the opposite one. When I'm asked to think on the spot, I get those 2 mixed up. When I think of them I have to picture them in my head before I can work out which is which. I also never know the names of streets in Crieff even though I have lived here since 1978. I know the street names and often look at their name signs as I walk past but never remember them and have to picture things on them to get them into my head. I have to picture the road and it's direction in my head to even get the main streets like the High Street and King Street, even though I know them well I still make the wee picture of them in my head when I think of them.

Telling you about getting an older girl at school to tie my laces for me, reminded me about my youngest brother Calum. He spent many years of his childhood with his laces undone. One day I sat him down and watched him tie his laces to see where he was going wrong. It turned out that he was doing it all right except for one bit where he was doing the right thing but upside down, so the laces tied but soon came out. We worked through it and he could do them fine after that.

Calum was also quite old when he still didn't hold or use a knife and fork properly. In fact it took a holiday to Sue's Dad and Step Mum, for him to learn how to do that. It is interesting to see the differences between Calum and Findlay, my 2 younger brothers and myself and Christopher and Duncan, my 2 older brothers. We all share the same Dad but Sue is Findlay and Calum's Mum.

I think perhaps in these cases that both Calum and I may just not have had a person taking the time out to teach us properly and watch that we actually had it right? Dad was busy working, when I was young and although we had loads of fun perhaps he didn't take time to do things with me like checking I could tie my shoe laces or tell the time?

When Sue came along she was, once married, very strict. (Dad was always very strict as well in those days but in a different way. When Dad got angry you knew to get well out the way or he would ask you something horrible like 'let me see your homework'. If we were doing the dusting he would sometimes run his finger along the skirting board to check if there was any dust. It's hard to believe he was like that nowadays when I look back on it. He is so cheery and laid back, a lovely, fun person.) Sue made us eat and use our knife and fork properly. If we had something like peas we were not allowed to scoop them onto the fork with the knife. We had to put the knife down and swap the fork into the right hand, scooping the peas up that way, which is not easy have you ever tried it?!! Calum didn't get that strictness, Findlay had no problem but we were all still at home for a while as Findlay was young, perhaps he picked up on those 'lessons'?

Findlay and Calum are both very clever. Findlay is verging on genius in a lot of things, he got loads of prizes at school but then so did all my brothers. Even I got the prize for Biology in 3rd year!

I would have got the Art prize that year too if the Art Department had done things the way the rest of the school did. In those days you got the prize for a subject if you got the highest mark in the whole year. I got that in Art but knew the Art Department didn't give prizes out very much. We were in the room of the head of the Art Department for something, so

I asked him if they were giving a prize out for that year, as I had not heard anything about it. He just said 'why, do you think you deserve it?' I was really embarrassed and wished I had kept my mouth shut.

Not so many years ago, my eldest brother Christopher told me about the comment that my Art teacher, Mr Kirley, made to my Dad at my parents night. Apparently he told Dad, 'Duncan is really good at Art but Blanche, Blanche is brilliant'. Dad never told me. Mr Kirley must have wondered why I was so cool about it after the parents' night. If I had heard that, I would have been much more confident and keen to go on and do Art. I so wish Dad had told me and that I had gone to Art College.

One lovely comment like that can really affect me. I seem to always need confirmation. Praise of good work is a huge motivation for me. The opposite can happen as well, I remember being really proud when I did a drawing of a wizard out of my head without copying anything. I loved it. Then Dad told me that Sue had said that the hands looked like lumps of wood, I crumpled it up and threw it in the bin.

Dad says that his Mum spent his whole childhood praising him for everything, so much so, that he didn't believe it. So I think he must have held back on praise for me and my big brothers, although he was different by the time Findlay and Calum came along. Back in the earlier days I did a painting of a Pink Floyd (I think) album cover of my big brothers. It turned out brilliant. I was really pleased with it. I must have gone on a bit too much though. I think I said something like it is exactly like the cover, as I can remember Dad saying 'I can see things wrong with it'. Again my confidence and elation were squashed. (I've finally found it on the internet it isn't Pink Floyd, it is King Crimson, "In the Court of the Crimson King".

Another comment I always remember is when I was in Primary School. At assembly we were all sitting, singing along to hymns. I used to really love that. There was one hymn I really loved that no one else seems to remember, it was something about, 'when a knight won his spurs in the battles of old, he was valiant and brave, he was gallant and bold.' Anyway this day I was singing along when Margo Polson, who was sitting next to me said 'do you have to sing'!!!! I was heartbroken and very embarrassed. Ever since then I sing very quietly when in a crowd and often just mime the song. I do really love singing though. I love music with a good beat and words that I can sing along to. I sing loudly and happily when listening to my music collection at home.

Anyway back to the Art department, they obviously didn't do the prizes the same way as the rest of the school but I was still stunned and ecstatic about my Biology prize. Dad and Sue even came to the prize ceremony. It was summer and always very hot and stuffy in that assembly hall. Sue was pregnant with Calum at the time and got taken out of the ceremony as she wasn't feeling well.

Findlay and Christopher (there are 17 years between them) come from the same family but grew up in very different situations and apart from the last couple of years of High School went to completely different schools and lived in different places. I find it extremely interesting that they both have very similar handwriting and very different from the rest of us:

Chris' Handwriting   **Findlays' Handwriting**

I find my 'picture head', as I call it, fascinating. I think that I see words as pictures and wonder if then I have more difficulty with words that can't have pictures. I was trying to think of an example then and looked at the word 'have' but then I realised that for have, I picture 2 hands handing over something. For 'to' I see or say in my head 2 then see the number 2, then see either the letters of the word two or to. For too I would have to sit and think now what is too for, I had to do it there, stop and think now what is too? Oh yes it means too much, I think I sort of thought of to and then added the oo seeing it sort of grow and 'heard' the word too with an emphasised oo in my head. So that whole process would take quite a while to do and is definitely not something I could do quickly if someone was pressing me for an answer.

I have taken some notes of examples of my 'funny' head over time as I have noticed them.

An interesting one was when I was doing an anagram I couldn't get the name, which was Flash Gordon, but I knew that was the answer! I could see him and was trying to work out his name as I knew that was the answer to the anagram. So my picture head can get the answer before my word head can.

This can cause muddles for example I have no idea of which is which with Arnold Swartzaneger and Sylvestor Stalone. If I think about it, I can picture a plastic faced sort of man, with a tan and muscles but I still don't know which person the picture is and think that I mix up both of them in a picture.

I have a wee bit that I cut out of a magazine as an example of the short cuts my head makes that can cause me trouble:

I looked at that again and wondered why I had kept it and what had muddled me about it. Then I realised that I was making the same mistake again. What catches my eyes, in that advert, is that it is from Marks and Spencers!! But of course it is nothing to do with Marks and Spencers. So my head must just look at the shapes really quickly and make up its mind what it says from the shapes?

Tom, who owns my flat, is a genius when it comes to words. He can get the conundrum in Countdown (a television quiz game) as soon as it turns over at times. Findlay and Tom are both brilliant at anagrams but I understand that. What I don't understand, is how he can get an anagram before I even have time to look at the letters, never mind have time to read them? It seems impossible to me. It suggests to me that he has a different way of reading, looking at and processing words and letters.

Tom did use to use shorthand when he worked as a journalist. I wonder if that has in someway trained his head to quickly look at and decipher shapes for words in some way? But then you would think that if that was the case, that my picture head would be better at anagrams than a word head, it isn't!

As for hearing new words I can't get them. I don't really have any idea what the person is saying. The way I find to help this is to get it spelt out, doing that, somehow I know where to start and it makes sense for me. This would happen with a name. It is much easier if someone writes a new name down for me. I do get names but if they are new, I would have to hear them a lot to get them.

So my communication and processing does seem to be quite different from a lot of people. Although **without** lots of people thinking about, discussing and describing the way that they do and deal with these things it is hard to tell just how different and what exactly those differences are. See another reason why more of you need to write a 'Living Diagnosis' book.

Chapter 4

In A Boy Beyond Reach, Cheri Florance discusses thinking in associations (visual) not sequences. I think this fits in with the way I think and how my thoughts jump in a way that makes no sense to others. They will be talking about something and what they say brings a picture to my head. That picture will make me think of something else but if I mention the new thing, they just look at me or stop, silent and completely stunned at why I suddenly brought that up.

I find it hard to concentrate on things unless I really get into them and then I am completely immersed in that world. I already mentioned how when I get 'lost' in book, I actually hear and see the scene. I remember at a party once, my Dad's 60th I think, the sitting room was packed with visitors, friends and neighbours. I was sitting down on the floor my head about chest level with my wee brother Calum, sitting next to me on a chair.

I was doing one of those sliding tile puzzles. I used to love them as a kid I did them non stop those ones with numbers that you had to slide into order and the harder (I thought) ones with letters. Anyway we had this puzzle at home like that only much harder with numbers on a dice (I think) that had to be put in rows alternately black and white and all the rows with each different number in it. It was really hard and I don't think any of us had ever done the puzzle over all the years that it had been in the house.

I also loved the rubiks cube when I was younger and found it a very satisfying feeling working with it. I never managed to do it but I did get the book with a solution in it and used to sit and do that over and over. Christopher actually managed to do the rubiks cube, that still really impresses me, although he always says 'it was only once', but I tried that often I know it was not something that could be just done by mistake, well maybe by a very, very extreme chance. (In recent years I heard C J on Eggheads, another television quiz show, saying that the rubiks cube is easy, you just have to look at the fixed centre square on each face and match the colours of each side to that. I thought this made such sense and so went out to find and buy a rubiks cube again. I love to have a wee go with the rubiks cube while using the computer when waiting for something to load or anything that is taking it's time. I have actually now managed to complete the rubiks cube myself 3 times, it is just luck really in that I just get as close as I can and carry on and on and those few times it has worked out much to my delight.)

Anyway I was sitting in this packed sitting room lost in the world of this puzzle. Calum must have leant forward in his seat to talk to someone. His voice suddenly burst into my wee world. I got such a fright I screamed loudly and dropped the puzzle. Then had to, extremely red faced, apologise and mutter a very strange sounding explanation to a room of silent, staring guests!!

That story was about the way I get lost in my own wee world but while writing it I realised what a good example it was of my inability to fit in with others' ways of socialising. I hate wasting 'good' time sitting in a room of people just talking. When we have family gatherings at home I love it when we all play board games. I love board games but not just sitting there for ages talking unless that talking is one to one about me or something I am interested in. I even hate when we are playing something like Trivial Pursuit and they start having a big long discussion about a subject that was in the question. I just want to get on.

My family are beginning to get used to my funny ways now, how I like to get home early. Although I think they all still have the 'what's wrong with Blanche' conversation when I'm not there. I remember one time starting a big jigsaw at a family party which I loved and it passed away the hours brilliantly. Nowadays I tend to play with the wee kids, which looks quite good cause it keeps them occupied and stops them annoying the 'adults'. It has its drawbacks though, the adults tend to think of me as a kid even though I am now getting rather too many decades old!

When reading books about peoples' lives with such things as autistic spectrum conditions etc, I like to note down any ideas or thoughts that really ring a bell with me. One such book I was reading was Only a Mother Could Love Him by Ben Polis.

It is a book about the author's life with ADHD, his struggle, self-taught concentration techniques and determination to get through the education system all the way to a degree. He couldn't get the book published but knew it was good. Followers of fashion won't look at different or new things and ways of looking at the world. (That statement doesn't make sense as followers of fashion are all about new things and ideas but it is perhaps just another example of the Emperors' New Clothes? The fashion has to be started first by fashion type experts!!) Ben ended up self-publishing the book. It was then taken up by other companies and became an international best seller.

He talks about 'being part of the book', just like I have been describing to you. He discusses deserving respect. I feel that, in the way that people don't seem to understand me nor take me seriously. I think because I am strange, look at things differently or say things unexpected that it is impossible for people to take me seriously it also kills conversations so things go silent. I think these things also stop me saying things so that I must seem like I don't want to talk. This is only a problem in serious or work situations, mostly people love my ways and I am good at cheering people up or making them laugh (in a nice way).

He mentions believing he is the best even if he is not. I always feel that I have a very arrogant view about myself and my place in the world. As I talked about before, I was not in the slightest bit interested in looking over and over again at other peoples' research in my studies. I just wanted to come up with my own views and ideas. I feel that I can do things and know things, I am right and of course when people don't agree then they just don't get it! But in another way I am very unconfident, I don't really feel that I fit in with other people, am no good at a lot of things that other people are good at and in the rest of the world (as opposed to my world) at times, I just don't get it.

I have discussed my inability to listen to lectures, taking them in, at the same time as taking notes. Ben discusses how he didn't have the concentration to write things down.

He writes 'it will be fine, it always is'. This is exactly my way of looking at things. I told you about the £1000 I got, right when I really needed it. Have trust and faith. I don't know if it was subconsciously to do with my Mum dying when I was young, but I always remember even when really young, that I would say to myself 'the worst thing that can happen is that I can die'. Meaning that it would be alright, it could never get too bad and I could cope.

He also says how he always felt lucky and that someone is 'looking out for' him. I know and believe this. I am an extremely positive, cheery person to the point that I expect it must drive a lot of people crazy!

Ben discusses how 'routine is vital for ADD/ADHD'. Well I am the queen of routine. People laugh at and tease me for my routines, in a nice way. But I love them and have them. Sometimes I think that I should break my routines and live life wildly or dangerously. Maybe it would do me the world of good and really help me, making life much more exciting. But I like my routines. They help me to look after myself. They are things that I have found that help to relax me or get the things that need doing done, or help me fix problems. For instance my routine of going for a nice warm bubble bath, then going to bed and reading my book before going to sleep, really helps me relax and get to sleep. This solves the problem of me needing a lot of sleep and **not** being able to switch off and get to sleep. The trouble comes when outside influences change my routines and then my system and body get messed up and confused.

Back in the book, Ben Polis, talks about how he couldn't believe how many people thought he was 'dumb'. Well I sort of have that problem but mostly with my family, not really thinking I'm stupid but probably just comparing me with all my brothers who do and did a lot better than me in exams and with General Knowledge etc.

As my Dad says about me, there are huge gaps in my General Knowledge but I do know the strangest things. I find incredible the amount of stuff that is in my head, I just can't get it out!! I always say that I need a new wee filing man in my head. Which for me conjures up images of the Numsculs or whatever they were called, do you remember them? I think they were in The Beano or maybe the Dandy? They were wee men that lived inside a person and sorted and got all the body systems working right.

In games like Trivial Pursuit sometimes I know that I know the answer but just can't get it out of my head. In that case I ask for the initials and then, if I do know it, I can get the answer. My wee brother Findlay says that is cheating but to me it is just a help getting what is in my head out. If I don't know it then I won't get it with the initials so it doesn't matter. It just equals my chances, not putting me ahead of the others.

I liked, when I was studying, when I worked out that Equal Opportunities was really 'equalling' opportunities, so you are not giving people advantages, you are providing them with support or access in order that they can start at the same level as other people, on an even footing.

Ben Polis talks about how encouragement is the only way to get through to ADHD students. Well I definitely need praise and am extremely motivated by praise and constantly need reassurance, acceptance and to have people realise that I am good at whatever it is.

He discusses how libraries and their quiet allow a student to isolate themselves. I can't read or listen when other people are about or waiting for me to do so. Quiet and no distractions can allow me to 'get lost' in the world of what I am doing. Although I must say that, apart from when reading, I get quite bored with complete quiet and like my music to be playing as long as it is my noise and under my control.

According to Ben most ADHD are visual learners, I think this fits in with my picture head. Although I actually think it depends on what I am to learn, I also find that I really need to try a thing for it to get into my head so it becomes real.

Fitting in with what I discussed earlier, he mentions difficulty getting to sleep with his mind never stopping. This fits in exactly with me not being able to switch off and the scenes playing over in my head if I have been at a family gathering or night out.

He discusses hyperfocussing and discusses 'laziness' like me but goes on to discuss how he has so many thoughts it is hard to finish anything. That definitely fits in with me starting and being really enthusiastic about so many things but then moving on to the next thing and the next excitement of a new project and creative adventure. I also fit in with his point that they can't motivate themselves to do the project that is me down to a tee.

He mentions in his book that you can get non-angry/violent ADD. That fits in with me. Although I do have a terrible temper, I can feel the blood all going to my head and I explode. But I hardly ever get like that, in fact in the last couple of decades I don't really remember getting angry much at all. That could be of course that I have got my own freedom and have been able to hide away from people. It was when my Dad used to try to tell me what to do or frustrated me with making his point which was the exact opposite of mine. I couldn't and can't get my point of view out into words especially if I really have to or if people are waiting for me to do so. I would also cry very easily in situations with my Dad when I was frustrated and trying to do what he wanted or state my case but couldn't get my point across. I think I am still very fragile that way, although again I don't have to face that kind of situation much at all nowadays. So it is frustration and also someone else trying to take control, therefore me losing my own control, which gets me furious. I still think that nowadays I am a very, very much more laid back and calmer person and that it would take a lot more for me to get angry like that now.

However just a year or so ago my big brother Chris was home and he still talks to me like the wee sister I always was to him, telling me not to be so whatever and what I should do. We were at a family gathering and I was telling my Dad that someone should phone Calum and invite him to an outing. I didn't want him to miss out. But Chris shouted at me to stop telling everyone what to do. Well I exploded at him in front of everyone. I think it always gives people a fright as I am usually such a quiet, hiding away kind of person. I was furious, frustrated and angry. He said that I could call Calum myself but I didn't want to do that as I knew Sue would have thought that I was interfering. I couldn't tell Chris that in front of everyone so I became frustrated and roared, my only way to deal with the situation.

The difference though was that now I could think about that and why it had happened. Afterwards, I said in front of everyone, 'Chris' you and I are going to have to start being able to talk to each other without shouting, we manage to do that with everyone else'. It was true and seemed to work as we now seem to both respect each other a lot more and are getting on great again. But perhaps it is just because everyone is nice to me or I avoid them that I just don't have to deal with those kinds of situations anymore?

Perhaps that is also why I can at times be driven to tears in social situations as my frustration and lack of control can't come out as shouting socially. I still find family times like Christmas, although brilliant and I love them, really stressful and often have really strange dreams leading up to them. I always seem to end up having a secret cry, to poor, good old Dad, about something that has upset me at these times. I try so hard that I get extra frustrated and upset if things don't go 'right'. As soon as I've had a cry, my head kind of drains down the sides of blood and I feel good again and can go off and be my usual cheery, jokey self again.

I really enjoyed Ben Polis' book. Not only did it ring a lot of bells and was interesting and a story of someone's life which I love to read but he also wrote the book and couldn't get it published. No one was interested. Then after he had sent it to loads of people, it was picked up by one who saw the magic and its worth and they published it. This is what I feel about my work, art, photography, writing, it isn't what 'people' want. But what I wonder is, are there more of you out there, people who are different. Do you see things differently, do you feel and know how things are so simple and obvious and just can't understand why other people just don't get it?

Another book I was reading talked about when a boy was asked what he wanted to do with his life and he panicked. I have never known what I have wanted to do with my life although I have spent my life with plans, dreams and goals of things that I do want to do.

Chapter 5

Another book I enjoyed that really made me think was the amazing story
by Charlotte Moore about her sons George and Sam. Different from my
usual likes of books that tell the amazing ways and breakthroughs that
people have had in beating and curing 'problems'. This book just
describes the amazing world of autistic children growing up, the
strangeness, magic and tears and joys.

She describes how guilt is a very non-autistic emotion. Dad has loads of
guilt and concerns about lying, he blames it on the strict Baptist church in
his youth but I very much doubt that. It seems much more likely that it is
our strangeness that means we find it very hard to lie. Perhaps that
seems to be a very strong care about doing right and not doing wrong to
other people. But perhaps it is a question of the definition of guilt? I
know that I have many times over the years said the truth about
something or rather in both Dad and my cases been 'blunt' about things
which is in fact much more autistic. We don't lie in that we must tell the
truth, autistic people definitely can have that to a much more extreme
case in that they say or show what they feel never mind how it affects
others.

I am no angel by the way and do tell lies but would never want to lie and can't understand people that lie about simple things such as lying about a night out when they really just can't be bothered. I would definitely just say 'no I don't feel like it' or 'can't be bothered' I **won't** say I will do something if I don't think that I will.

Granny Haddow (Dad's Mum) used to say when someone died something like, 'oh well that's another one away then'. That is the sort of way I am, matter of fact, things are done and that's it.

That doesn't mean I don't feel things, indeed I feel things very strongly and am very affected by them and so probably try to avoid them. For instance if there is a horrible disaster on the news, I like to see the news and what has happened but that is it, then I switch it off. I hate the way the telly goes on and on about it making it into entertainment in a horrible kind of way. It's not because I don't care. It's because I feel it too much, I don't want all the images and thoughts to be made stronger and stronger.

Each night I watch the news headlines and if any story stands out or interests me I will watch the news until that comes on but usually the headlines are enough for me. Perhaps partly because of habits like this, I know vaguely what is going on in the world but I still have no idea of peoples names or what they do unless I hear and see them and their names a lot of times. This can be very embarrassing with strangers who don't realise that I've got such bad general knowledge. Mind you I think the name thing is because of my picture head. Just a sound or a word which is what a name is, doesn't stick with me nor get processed until or unless it is connected with a scene or person I have already experienced. Even then it would still work much better if repeated over and over.

Moore discusses how George and Sam don't thankfully suffer from Kanner's criterion of being motivated by a desire for the 'preservation of sameness'. Obviously I don't have this in any kind of autistic level way but it did make me think again of my 'wee routines'. How Helen and Dolores used to tease me about the way I laid my tray out ready each day at work with my juice, bit of chewing gum etc. I still do all that. Although I live what to some people might think was messily, I hate when someone moves something and doesn't put it back right. If I take something out of the cupboard to use, I hate and can't understand if Tom fills the space up with something else. It just doesn't make sense to me to do that.

I absolutely hated when Dad used to come to visit Tom sometimes to play scrabble and would move 'my' chair over to where he wanted it. It was like he came into my territory and took over. I love my Dad and I don't know why I am like this with him but I know it is something to do with me being in control here in my home and not wanting to lose that control. It is my safe place for me.

When Tom is due to come home to stay for a while, I have dreams about him changing things, adding things, redecorating etc. I actually end up quite enjoying his visits but then I know that to me when he is home that the flat is his and his territory. My bedroom is mine and I can cope with that, at least for a while.

Charlotte Moore discusses how an Asperger child 'can't accommodate a friend, unless that friend is prepared to obey his every command'! That reminded of me of when I went for a holiday to my Granny Haddow's. We were out in the garden and she said that she had found a friend for me to play with and looked over to a wee girl in the next garden. I said that I didn't want a friend and Granny said oh ok. I don't know what Granny or that wee girl thought of me but I remember getting on with my playing and being really relieved that I didn't have to play with the girl.

Later in the book Moore mentions Georges' 'lack of ability to edit or organize his memory'. This fits in with my need for a better 'filing man' in my head. Also with me knowing that I have so much stuff in my head but am not able to get it out when needed to answer a question, get a name etc. Perhaps again this is to do with a picture head instead of a word head, how can you bring a picture out as an answer to an on the spot question?

My friend Babs is always brilliant at telling me who someone is if someone says their name. I never know who they are from their name but Babs tells me a wee story or describes some memory of them so that I know exactly who they are. In fact Babs was always brilliant at understanding what I was going on about and would say to people, 'she means ...'.

People often don't know what I'm talking about which I can at times find very frustrating. I know what I just said has made perfect sense why don't they know what I mean? Often someone says something and I say 'oh so you mean ...' and they say 'no I mean ...' and then proceed to say exactly what I thought they meant! Perhaps it has something to do with my 'jumping head'. Perhaps I have jumped onto the next idea and they are still waiting for me to acknowledge their first idea?

Babs was always brilliant at knowing what I meant, 'understanding my language'. I was reminded of this just the other night, at a quiz night. I said something and her Mum commented on it and Babs answered for me 'no, she meant ...' and proceeded to say what I was meaning. Why don't they get what I say? Why does Babs make sense of me when others don't and why don't they? This all sounds as if I can't talk or something but believe me, I get on fine in a perfectly normal way, with normal speech and communication.

Chapter 6

When reading The Genesis of Artistic Creativity by Michael Fitzgerald I kept seeing bits like me in it. It is a book about famous creative people and their funny ways! For example Lewis Carroll like Bruce Chatwin would abruptly leave a gathering. As I have told you before I always like to 'get away home' and hate when I have to rely on or wait for someone else to give me a lift. As I don't yet drive, this is often a problem.

I had Fitzgerald's book sitting around in the sitting room for months and even though I had often talked about, looked at it and read it. It was not until I wrote the title down for the notes of this book that I actually realised the title is The Genesis and not Genius. I thought it was a book about geniuses so it made sense to be called that.

Sometimes I seem to go into a wee dream. Often I will be having a bath or doing something and suddenly realise that I was caught up in my thoughts and lost time. It doesn't last long it is just like suddenly waking up like in my books when I suddenly realise that the noise has stopped and the battle or whatever is over.

This can also happen in front of people but for a much shorter time. An example of this was when I was at an interview for Learning Resource Assistant at Crieff High School. I was answering a question when I suddenly realised that I was staring at a poster and had gone into a 'dwam'. I don't know if it is noticeable? No one ever says anything perhaps it only happens for a split second? I don't know if I actually go silent or not.

I also sometimes say 'oh sorry I was away in a wee dream' when someone says 'hello Blanche' to me in the street and I hadn't noticed them. I think that is a more common thing though isn't it?

A thing that I find fascinating is how hard it is to recognise someone with sunglasses on. I always used to think that it was stupid when a famous person would try to disguise themselves just by wearing sunglasses. But I saw a neighbour that I often see, one time in the street and didn't realise who she was until she said hello. The only thing different about her was that she had sunglasses on. I always think that I don't really look at people but that tells me that I must look at peoples' eyes a lot more than I realised I did.

They're amazing things eyes, occasionally I look at my eyes and realise that they are actually horrible things and have actual holes in them. But we see eyes as beautiful. It is amazing how we see things that we are used to as beauty. Like ladies with shaved legs and men with shaved chins even though it is not natural and is just what we are used to. Another thing that we don't mind at all that is actually a huge big horrible hole and scar, if you think about it, is our tummy button!

At school in science with good old Mr Cuthbert, we got to cut up bulls' eyes. That was in the days when you were still allowed to do fun things like cutting things up and didn't have to worry about all these stupid Health and Safety guidelines or being politically correct. I still remember cutting into the eye. It was really hard to cut into. When I did get in, a load of black fluid (blood?) came out. We were going to get to cut up a dead rabbit one day that a boy was bringing in. But that class was cancelled as the rabbit turned out to be riddled with fleas and Mr Cuthbert had to throw it out!

By the way I started talking about the bull's eyes because I was thinking about what eyes looked like. Perhaps I jumped a bit there, did I? That is how a picture head works.

Politically Correct can get really stupid. It is extremely important, I believe, not to be nasty about someone or something and using a name in a derogatory way is not good and should not be allowed. But it just gets stupid. Mind you it is true, that it is what you are used to, things and ways of saying things change and what was acceptable soon becomes horrible and sometimes I can't believe that I used to say it.

Chapter 7

As I have said a lot of us Haddows have our funny ways. I think we all like and need to be in control but that could be our upbringing, a big family, a strict (in those days) Dad and a need to be heard and noticed? But I also feel my need for control is my way to keep myself safe.

As I said my lovely nephew Jack has Asperger Syndrome. Jack and his Dad, my brother Chris, plan to write a book about Jack's experiences someday. So come on you two if I can do it you can too.

Dad is daft and crazy like the rest of us. He describes his Mum (Granny Haddow) as very strange in a lot of ways. It can be hard to know what ways to take some of Dads ideas as like me, he can have strange and different views about the way things should be and are. But it does seem that Granny Haddow was quite a character. Grampa Haddow seems to have been quite strict and from the way Dad describes it, despairing at times, of Dad. It would be interesting to hear it from Dad's brother's (Uncle Jack) point of view.

A story that springs to mind and that I can sympathise with and understand completely is the Mecas Mecas Mecas story. Sorry Dad if I got the word wrong but as you know I have trouble hearing what is said if it doesn't actually make any sense!

So Dad was sitting at the dinner table at home. They had said prayers before their meal for many years. This day, Grampa Haddow, decided that Norman (Dad) should say the prayer. Dad had been there as they said the prayer many, many times in his life. But when asked to say the prayer, he had no idea whatsoever what the words actually were. The closest he could get to it was 'Mecas, mecas, mecas'! Grampa was furious and certainly (from what Dad says) had no understanding or sympathy for Dad's strange ways. I can't remember exactly what the prayer was but I presume it was 'May the Lord **make us** Thankful'?

Christopher the eldest of us siblings is, like us all, a lovely, friendly, cheery, caring person. He is very intelligent although seems to have little confidence and self belief in his cleverness. I remember him getting the Chemistry prize at school but he doesn't seem to remember that. He went to Dollar Academy from the days when we were a richer, 'posher' family, who must have had less Liberal views about education.

It was only in very recent years that I learned that Christopher had a horrible time and was bullied at Crieff High School which he joined once we moved there in 1978. It did make me think back and I do remember that we did hate and were horrible to anyone who was 'posh'.

Chris mixed up writing b and d when he was young. He also like me said 'f' instead of 'th'. Sue thankfully taught me how to change that when still young but I can remember Christopher still saying that into his adulthood.

The next sibling is Duncan, a lovely, caring chap. He is a vegetarian, which he has been for many years. As a child he was great fun always into everything. Dad used to call him plunkin Duncan (he told me in recent years that he really hated being called that), as he would always take everything to pieces, not always able to put them back together again. He always wanted a vintage car and would save up his money in an old torch. The torch didn't work, but was a good store for money. One day he came back from the antiques shop with a big vintage car horn or hooter that he had saved up his money for.

Duncan had a terrible temper that we would occasionally see when things would be thrown about. One day in Olgivie Bank, the house we rented for a year when we first came to Crieff, he got into a rage about something. I can't remember what it was now, it could have been that he had made us a meal but none of us had come down to get it. Anyway he got very angry and exploded, throwing his pot of baked beans everywhere. We tidied it all up and were astonished later when Sue got home and the first thing she said was who has been throwing baked beans about?! It turned out that there were still baked beans on the ceiling above the washing pulley!!

A couple of years after that, when we had moved to our new house in Crieff, Findlay was born. A brilliant and lovely wee boy, he was born in 1980, in my summer holidays between Primary 7 and 1st year. We were all still at home and did a lot of looking after Findlay and got very close to him. Findlay must have been influenced a lot by being, in a way an only child, but also having 3 big teenage siblings.

Findlay loved water, he would play in water whenever he got the chance and was often caught playing with the toilet water!! If you ever lost anything you could usually find it, having been hidden by Findlay, in the washing machine! He was a very well behaved wee boy and would play for hours out exploring, playing bows and arrows etc. He later went on to play archery for the Scottish Junior team, later moving on to Volley ball and playing for the Scottish University team. He got loads and loads of medals, cups and awards over the years.

When wee he loved to make 'traps' and inventions, often you would go into a room only to find it all tied up with string and things connected to each other. His wee son Andrew seems to be following him now in that department. He also loved to sleep in different places, often making tents and a number of times having slept in the empty bath!

Findlay was one of those very rare people who not only excelled and got prizes in sports but also in academics. He is a lovely cheery all round friendly person who has kept his magic, youth and enthusiasm for life due in part, I believe, to his wife Mairi, who couldn't be more of a 'Haddow' if she tried!!

Four years after Findlay was born, the final Haddow sibling came along, Calum. The youngest of us, he is now the tallest and has the longest name, with a very grand 2 middle names!!

Calum is also a real character. He has developed a real wicked sense of humour, quite in line with Christopher's. Far too clever and 'horrible' for my taste! A friendly and great fun boy now man, Calum is again very different but most definitely a Haddow.

When wee he would love to watch his videos over and over again. From an early age if I tried to read him a bed time story, he would say, much to my annoyance, 'can I do the reading'. He is very good at English and like Duncan excels at music, both writing and playing his own songs.

He seemed, when young, to try and copy people, which he was very good at, but it didn't seem to be until his teenage years that he really developed into his own character with his own idiosyncratic ways. He always had a best friend and loads of friends. Findlay on the other hand was more of a person for general friends.

Calum also did very well at school also getting prizes. Living slightly in the shadow of Findlay's non-stop success Calum, like Duncan, became more of a joker. He was a very gentle boy and most like Dad in that way, I think than all of his brothers.

Sue is Sue and has been part of our family since she married Dad in 1977. As I have discussed, she is **not** fluent in Haddow 'language' and often seems to despair and be totally lost in our reasons for calling an item a 'wee scrapey thing' or such like!! Sue is also intelligent. She is a vegetarian, was, in the past, an active member in CND and has put up with and stuck with us all throughout the years.

Rather than our obsession for playing board games, Sue prefers to sit in the sitting room and read her papers, do the crosswords or watch tv. Calum also eventually got fed up with non-stop games and either retired to the sitting room or more usually went out to find whatever friend of his was also home for a family Christmas! Sue was a High school French/English teacher, which she gave up when pregnant to bring up her children, then becoming a child minder. In later years she went back to teaching, now in Primary. She has thrived there and became a Deputy Head although I know you don't call them that now, I've no idea what you do call them now.

So that is the family or at least some of them. There are also now Findlay's 2 lovely, brilliant kids (who seem to be, like their parents, extremely intelligent and also bright, wild and fun), Calum's 1 kid (who I don't know much about as he lives in Australia but he seems like a bright, cheery wee thing), Duncan's 2 children, grown up now and Chris' 2 other children from his second marriage, all also wee stars and real lovely characters. Christopher's youngest son, Chey, is severely autistic and still not speaking, as far as I know (they live in England at the moment and we haven't seen them for quite a few years now. Chey is getting to go to a special school now and seems to be doing well there). He seems a happy wee boy but completely in his own wee world. From about the age of 1 onwards I have felt he must be on the autistic spectrum. This wasn't diagnosed for quite a while. When it was, sadly his mum and sister had to move away from Christopher in the (UAE) United Arab Emirates in order to get Chey into a special school in England. When I used to see him each Summer and he was younger, he would eat things (anything) and twice I stupidly put my finger in his mouth to try and remove something. Well it was an extremely sore lesson for me. He seemed to have no idea about how I don't want my finger very heavily chomped on! When they came to Scotland from UAE for holidays in earlier years, Chey seemed to really love the wind, which he would stand and feel on his face. He got very upset at change but slowly got used to us on the holidays and loved going for walks. Poor Chris, his daughter Sienna, hated having to walk and son, Chey, hated when they stopped walking!!

I am very interested in the autistic spectrum and its very many connections. How much is autism connected with family and how many more 'conditions' such as dyslexia, dyspraxia, ADHD etc are connected. How many people from my generation and before have autistic spectrum type symptoms but will never know, nor ever have an official diagnosis? How many of the 'geeks' at school were really autistic, how many of the 'bad boys' were actually ADHD? And how many girls have these types of conditions but because of society and the ways our brains make us behave don't actually show it?

The Last Word

So this book is about exploration and thoughts. I am not saying what is right or wrong but what I believe in and know to be right now for me. Even as I wrote this book over time my views, ideas, thoughts and situation changed at times quite a lot.

I like to and try to respect other beliefs and ideas. The whole point of this book is to get people thinking. There are other ways, more answers. To grow, move and evolve in life we need to be free to think, learn, change, evolve and alter our ideas and beliefs as we go. Be open not closed. Listen and learn but also make up our own minds and believe what is right for ourselves.

I think we, as a society, often have a 'fear' of anything not proven, **not** scientific. Perhaps this is connected with and has a basis in Religion, to the 'witch hunts', giving us a fear of being different. But then I suppose it would never have worked in society to be different as then you would be outcast and miss out on whatever society provides us with.

As you will have seen from this book, I am different. Maybe lots of us are 'different', how many of us just pretend to fit in with everyone else? I don't know but I do know that it is all fascinating. Thank you for listening or reading and thinking. Perhaps it has made you look at yourself, something or someone in your own life differently?

As for the Autistic Spectrum, as you will have found out, I am fascinated with it and its possible connections. How many of you out there have Autistic Spectrum type conditions in yourself or family? Do you have connections with such things as dyslexia, ways of thinking, looking at things? Who is affected by these things? Which members of your family could be connected with this, are there any connections, could there be links, ideas we are missing? Why should we leave it all to the 'professionals'? We are living life. We can research it and experience it, its connections, wonders and strangeness all the time. What can we **each** learn from, explore and add to the thoughts and ideas?

So much could be discovered from **us** rather than set up clinical observations or small samples of society. So write your own book or respond with your own thoughts, feelings and views to this book and others like it. Let us all input into society and perhaps we can then start to all fit in, belong and feel comfortable and part of it no matter how different and individual we may be. Society is supposed to be a large group of people living in an organised way. Perhaps if we tell, learn and understand just how different we all are, then that in itself could bring us together and move us on to advance and evolve in a good and positive way.

As I've said, I am a caring, hopeful and optimistic kind of person. In trying to find new music lately that I like, one of the groups I found were the Dixie Chicks (who are not my favourite but okay). There is one song of theirs that I really like, I would like to leave you with the lyrics but I don't know if I am allowed to put them in the book? So instead I will give you a task to do, go and find this song put it on and listen to the words. Oh and people like Dad, give it a chance, don't just think it is a noise, you have to listen to it quite loud to enjoy it! The song is: *I Hope* sung by the Dixie Chicks. Go on give it a go.

References

Barbara Jacobs, *Loving Mr Spock, The Story of a Different Kind of Love*, (Penguin Books, 2003) ISBN 0718146425

Charlotte Moore, *George and Sam*, (Penguin Books, 2005) ISBN 0141014539

Polis Ben, *Only a Mother Could Love Him*, (Mobius, 2005) ISBN 0340838922

Fitzgerald Michael, *The Genesis of Artistic Creativity*, (Jessica Kingsley 2005) ISBN 1843103346

Myers Peter *et al*, *An Exact Mind and Artist With Asperger Syndrome*, (Jessica Kingsley 2004) ISBN 9781843100324

Kosinski Jerzy, *Being There*, (Grove Press 1999) ISBN 0802136346

Magazines

Chat Magazine, IPC Media

Gazette, November 2006, (CSB) Central Scotland Branch of the Dry Stone Walling Association

Websites

http://www.speakdolphin.com/home.cfm

http://www.idw.org/ (International Dolphin Watch Website)

https://www.facebook.com/BsPhotosWorld?fref=ts (Bs Photos my facebook photo blog)

http://bsphotographs.blogspot.com/ (B's Photos, a website of some of my photos taken on my walks.)

http://bspaintings.blogspot.com/ (B's Paintings, a website of some of my artwork.)

Made in the USA
Middletown, DE
28 September 2017